Digital Assets and the Limits of Czech Property Law

ACADEMIC PAPERS

Digital Assets and Limits of the Czech Property Law

Jana Soukupová

Wolters Kluwer

Citation:
Jana Soukupová. *Digital Assets and Limits of Czech Property Law* (Kluwer Law International 2025)

Review: JUDr. Bc. Zdeněk Kučera, Ph.D.

Published by:
Kluwer Law International B.V.
PO Box 316
2400 AH Alphen aan den Rijn
The Netherlands
E-mail: lrs-sales@wolterskluwer.com
Website: www.wolterskluwer.com/en/solutions/kluwerlawinternational

Sold and distributed by:
Wolters Kluwer Legal & Regulatory U.S.
920 Links Avenue
Landisville, PA 17538
United States of America
E-mail: customer.service@wolterskluwer.com

ISBN 978-94-035-4109-9
e-Book: ISBN 978-94-035-4119-8
web-PDF: ISBN 978-94-035-4129-7

TABLE OF CONTENT

ABOUT THE AUTHOR

Jana Soukupová works as a junior associate at Dentons law firm and as a lecturer at the Center for Law, Technology, and Digitalization at the Faculty of Law of Charles University in Prague. She was a member of the research team for the TAČR project Legal Aspects of Virtual and Augmented Reality. For her doctoral research, she received a SYLFF scholarship, which enabled her to complete research stays at Maastricht University and Queen Mary University of London. In her practice, she focuses on ICT law, personal data protection, and intellectual property law.

LIST OF ABBREVIATIONS[1]

ABGB or Austrian civil code	Allgemeines bürgerliches Gesetzbuch für die gesammten deutschen Erbländer der Oesterreichischen Monarchie StF: JGS Nr. 946/1811, as amended
Czech Civil Code	Act no. 89/2012 the Civil Code, as amended
Czech Commercial Code	Act 90/2012 on Commercial Companies and Cooperatives, as amended
Consumer Rights Directive	Directive 2011/83/EU of the European Parliament and of the Council of 25 October 2011 on consumer rights, amending Council Directive 93/13/EEC and Directive 1999/44/EC of the European Parliament and of the Council and repealing Council Directive 85/577/EEC and Directive 97/7/EC of the European Parliament and of the Council Text with EEA relevance
Copyright Act	Act no. 121/2000 on Copyright and Rights Related to Copyright and on an Amendment to Certain Acts (the Copyright Act), as amended
Digital Content Directive	Directive (EU) 2019/770 of the European Parliament and of the Council of 20 May 2019 on certain aspects concerning contracts for the supply of digital content and digital services
BGB or German civil code	Bürgerliches Gesetzbuch in der Fassung der Bekanntmachung vom 2. Januar 2002 (BGBl. I S. 42, 2909; 2003 I S. 738), as amended
GDPR	Regulation (EU) 2016/679 of the European Parliament and of the Council of 27 April 2016 on the protection of natural persons with regard to the processing of personal data and on the free movement of such data, and repealing Directive 95/46/EC (General Data Protection Regulation) (Text with EEA relevance)
IP	Intellectual property

[1] Unless otherwise stated, all regulations cited in the text are used as amended.

Sale of Goods Directive	Directive (EU) 2019/771 of the European Parliament and of the Council of 20 May 2019 on certain aspects concerning contracts for the sale of goods, amending Regulation (EU) 2017/2394 and Directive 2009/22/EC, and repealing Directive 1999/44/EC
MiCA	Regulation (EU) 2023/1114 of the European Parliament and of the Council of 31 May 2023 on markets in crypto-assets, and amending Regulations (EU) no. 1093/2010 and (EU) no. 1095/2010 and Directives 2013/36/EU and (EU) 2019/1937 (Text with EEA relevance)

INTRODUCTION

In the past two decades we have observed several attempts to apply traditional property law to that which is digital and intangible. This is a mere result of the fact that the consumer choice has shifted from owning to accessing. Accordingly, we are observing a significant rise in services offering access to libraries full of movies, TV series, books, videogames, and music. Additionally, a similar trend is evident of people tending to invest heavily in assets without physical form, such as Bitcoins or NFTs. Our lives have become flooded with virtual accounts encompassing a variety of uses. Such accounts typically hold something of value to users. This can be either a virtual representation of something purchased by us, such as a sword in an online game, or these accounts may have a particular value for us in their mere existence. For influencers, value may be derived from the number of followers that generate revenue or boost sponsorship deals. For casual users, such value may lie in the simple fact that the given account stores our memories in the form of photographs and personal messages. Additionally, many objects that still preserve their physical form, such as various wearables, are now equipped with a layer of code that enhances them for our everyday use, e.g. smart watches.[1]

The shift from the real to the virtual has brought many challenges, including how law could or should address this transition. In the past decade, we have seen a host of successful or failed attempts to apply current legal norms to what is digital and intangible. For example, in 2012 a Dutch court concluded that a sword in an online game had value as it represented time and energy and thus may be a subject to theft.[2] Recently, the concept that Bitcoin can be considered property was affirmed in England, but not in Japan.[3] Or that one may freeze an NFT because some proprietary rights apply to them.[4] And finally, a Dutch court recently ruled that data files cannot be owned because they are intangible; however, the computer with the data may be reivindicated.[5]

---

1 PERZANOWSKI, Aaron a Jason M SCHULTZ. *The End of Ownership: Personal Property in the Digital Economy*. Cambridge: The MIT Press, 2016. ISBN 0-262-33596-4, p. 191.

2 Teen steals virtual items, gets real punishment. *CBS.* [online] 31. 1. 2012 [Accessed 2023-07-20]. Available at: https://www.cbsnews.com/news/teen-steals-virtual-items-gets-real-punishment/.

3 Judgement of High Court of England from 2019, AA v Persons Unknown, EWHC 3556 English High Court and GULLIFER, Louise. English translation of the Mt Gox judgment on the legal status of bitcoin prepared by the Digital Assets Project. [online]. 11. 2. 2019 [Accessed 2023-07-20]. Available at: https://www.law.ox.ac.uk/business-law-blog/blog/2019/02/english-translation-mt-gox-judgment-legal-status-bitcoin-prepared.

4 Judgement of High Court of England from 2023, Lavinia Deborah Osbourne v Persons Unknown Category A & Ors [2023] EWHC 39.

5 Judgement of the Netherlands Commercial Court from 21 April 2023, NCC 22/018.

All of the above are currently just bits and pieces of judicial ruling spread across multiple jurisdictions. Yet, there are representations of a similar trend — one aligned with our lives being increasingly tethered to the digital world and becoming dependent on things we usually do not own or control (or for which the law does not allow ownership), since access to them is in the power of companies that provide these services. This can be termed a **relativisation of traditional property**.

Consequently, instead of owning we now only access various accounts and assets online and the rights to these assets are heavily governed via the terms of services of these platforms. This fact has led to the creation of a body of legal literature responding to the aforementioned changes in our society. Such legal literature (and the law itself) had to deal with a new phenomenon that could be described as "everything digital". Notions like virtual property, digital assets, smart property, res digitales, digital content, or simply digital objects began to appear. At this point, the debate covers everything from the ownership of virtual objects, such as videogame objects or Internet accounts, to the legal implications of the Internet of Things.[6] And although it is evident that such authors focus on the rights associated with digital objects and describe the same phenomenon, it was not always apparent whether these objects are (or even should be) part of the same debate since the debate has become increasingly fragmented.[7]

Alongside the newly appearing terminology, a body of literature arguing that we are losing our property rights has also been evidenced. Natalie Banta even called the current state a "digital feudalism".[8] Similarly, Joshua Fairfield observed that ownership is "*under attack and fading fast.*"[9] In addition authors Perzanowski and Schulz talk about "*aggressive intellectual property laws, restrictive contractual provisions, and technological locks that have weakened end user control over the digital goods we acquire.*"[10] As a result, we can find strong calls for change, such as a reforms of copyright laws[11], changes in consumer laws[12] or reform of property laws.[13]

---

6 FAIRFIELD, Joshua. *Owned: Property, Privacy, and the New Digital Serfdom.* Cambridge: Cambridge University Press, 2017, p. 49–76; PERZANOWSKI, Aaron a Jason M SCHULTZ. *The end of ownership: Personal property in the digital economy.* Cambridge: The MIT Press, 2016. ISBN 0-262-33596-4, pp. 139–154.

7 Comp. PAŁKA, Przemysław. *Virtual Property — Towards a General Theory.* 2017, pp. 104–106.

8 BANTA, Natalie M. Property interests in digital assets: the rise of digital feudalism. *Cardozo law review* [online]. Cardozo School of Law, 2017, 38(3), 1099 [Accessed 2023-02-03]. ISSN 0270-5192.

9 FAIRFIELD, Joshua. *Owned: Property, Privacy, and the New Digital Serfdom.* Cambridge: Cambridge University Press, 2017, p. 13.

10 PERZANOWSKI, Aaron a Jason M SCHULTZ. *The End of Ownership: Personal Property in the Digital Economy.* Cambridge: The MIT Press, 2016. ISBN 0-262-33596-4, p. 4.

11 Ibid., p. 178.

12 Ibid., p. 174

13 ERP, Sjef van. Ownership of Data: The Numerus Clausus of Legal Objects. *Brigham-Kanner Property Rights Conference Journal.* 2017, vol. 6. Revised and expanded version, p. 21–23; FAIRFIELD, Joshua. *Owned: Property, Privacy, and the New Digital Serfdom.* Cambridge: Cambridge University Press, 2017, pp. 236–244.

It is important to note that the property debate, which has strong roots in the common law, has not been recognized by the European legislator. Although the topic of digital assets is currently receiving a lot of international attention, mostly due to the UNIDROIT Principles on Digital Assets and Private Law, the EU has decided to choose another regulatory path. Thus, instead of applying property law regimes, we were introduced with platform regulations such as DSA or DMA, consumer regulations as the Digital Content Directive, or data governance regulation such as the Data Act and Data Governance Act. And finally, we were introduced with cryptoassets regulation — MiCA. All of the mentioned regulations apply to digital assets to a certain degree and to access to data to certain extent. Yet, the existence of this new regulations does not negate that within individual jurisdiction, property law may still be relevant for digital assets.

Despite of digital assets being subject to many regulations, this monograph focuses only on property law questions of digital assets. Specifically, this book will address the terminological issues surrounding digital assets and their legal nature under private law. The main aim of this work is to answer the question what the limits of Czech property rights are concerning digital assets. In other words, how digital assets conceptually fit into the body of Czech property law, and specifically into the Czech Civil Code. As noted, a host of literature focuses on the concept of property and its relevance in today's digital world. This book will thus focus on the application of the current Czech property-related legal framework (with a focus on ownership and possession) concerning digital assets and observe whether room exists for an analogy, or rather if "control" over digital assets and "access" to them are separate phenomena that the current Czech legal framework is presently unable to accommodate.

This monograph is not designed to be a regulatory paper calling for reforms of a certain field of law — at least not in the sense that its purpose is to offer an argument about the need to strengthen users' "property" rights in cyberspace. Similarly, this work is not designed to be a conceptual work on property rights in general as it focuses predominantly on Czech law. This work does also not address the topic of personal data protection, consumer law or financial law, even though these topics are also connected to digital assets.

The introduction to this book aims to outline lingering questions concerning how the current body of property law applies in cyberspace and whether laws should be adapted to better regulate this field. No consensus or clear legal framework has yet been developed concerning digital assets. For some countries this means that none of their laws can be used for offering legal protections in this respect. Moreover, legislators are being tasked with regulating the respective legal issues surrounding data, digital assets, digital content and the like while trying to avoid overlapping proposals or changing hundreds of years of existing legal systems. The result is incoherent regulation such as the Digital Content Directive which, on the one hand, introduces a legal regime for digital content and digital services while, on the other, leaves unanswered how digital content or digital services fit into the existing legal system or the differences between them. Moreover, calls have been heard to regulate the legal regime surrounding data, digital assets and cryptoassets without a clear understanding of what these notions even mean. Thus, an understanding is required of just how complex the online world has become, how the digital economy functions, along with basic definitions of data, digital assets and similar concepts, as well as whether one can truly own these. This understanding is crucial for legislators to address this ever-evolving technological reality.

Multiple reasons can be found why the topic of digital assets and property rights are important. As of now, digital assets are an umbrella term that encompasses numerous digital intangibles, some of which are protected as intellectual property, as well as others that do not fit within this framework. Accordingly, the question of which protection is required for which digital assets, and whether traditional property concepts can be applied, is of utmost importance. Secondly, classifying some assets as property or a thing has legal consequences. If a digital asset is a thing or property, it might lead to the consequence that it may be a subject to a trust fund, part of matrimonial assets or be inherited. It may also mean that it is part of insolvency assets or that one may, as a beneficiary, authorise another person to manage digital assets as a part of a property management arrangement. There may also be instances when granting someone a proprietary protection is necessary. As addressed above, the courts recently recognized cryptoassets as property for the purposes of a proprietorial injunction on several occasions. Finally, traditional property is strictly jurisdiction dependant. What may be a property under common law may not be deemed property under German law or Polish law or Czech law, as an example. This may lead to people having unequal rights to their digital assets depending on the respective jurisdiction.

The law surrounding digital assets is incredibly complex. As the following chapters will unveil, even such a thing as drawing a simple line between data, digital assets or cryptoasstets is not an easy task. And when it comes to property law applicable to these digital intangibles, there is even a bigger theoretical divide. This mean that every attempt to apply property law or criticize such application will always be perceived by some as imperfect or wrong. But this is exactly what makes this topic perfect for endless discussions about our perception of property and all rights and values we see under this category.

1 MAPPING THE FIELD OF DIGITAL ASSETS

1.1 What are Digital Assets?

Defining digital assets is not an easy task, chiefly for two main reasons. Firstly, in most countries digital assets are not a legal notion or a legal category. This does not mean that the meaning of digital assets cannot be classified according to the law. However, the definition of digital assets is usually "borrowed" from other fields, and no common consensus exists on what the term should cover.

Secondly, many other similar notions have appeared in literature over the years. For example, authors Fairfield[1] or Lastowka and Hunter[2] coined the term "*virtual property*" which is another notion tied to digital intangibles. Their respective understanding of virtual property, however, slightly differs. Fairfield defines the term as "*rivalrous, persistent, and interconnected Code*".[3] Lastowka and Hunter, on the other hand, as "*entries in a database resident on a server that permits a participant's computer monitor to display images already present within the software.*"[4] Although the underlying idea that virtual property is some sort of code is the same, the attributes of such code under these two definitions differ. For Fairfield, virtual property is characterized by its proprietary nature (i.e., being rivalrous, persistent and interconnected). Lastowka and Hunter, on the other hand, only seek to describe the technical reality behind the code.

Moreover, in the ensuing years Fairfield devised a few other terms such as "*smart property*"[5] and "*digital property*".[6] On top of that, we find terms such as "*virtual goods*"[7] or "*virtual items*"[8] in various legal literature. The meaning behind

---

1 FAIRFIELD, Joshua. Virtual Property. *Boston University Law Review*. 2005, vol. 85, no. 4.
2 LASTOWKA, Greg — HUNTER, Dan. The Laws of the Virtual Worlds. *California Law Review*. 2004, vol. 92, no. 1.
3 FAIRFIELD, Joshua. Virtual Property. *Boston University Law Review*. 2005, vol. 85, no. 4, p. 1053.
4 LASTOWKA, Greg — HUNTER, Dan. The Laws of the Virtual Worlds. *California Law Review*. 2004, vol. 92, no. 1, p. 40.
5 FAIRFIELD, Joshua. *Owned: Property, Privacy, and the New Digital Serfdom*. Cambridge: Cambridge University Press, 2017, p. 16.
6 Ibid.
7 ENG, Kenneth W. Content Creators, Virtual Goods: Who Owns Virtual Property. *Cardozo Arts & Entertainment Law Journal*. 2016, vol. 34, no. 1.
8 PAŁKA, Przemysław. *Virtual Property — Towards a General Theory*. 2017.

these notions will be further explored in Chapter 3. The overview of the notions here is only intended to illustrate the terminological complexity of the topic.

As for the notion of digital assets, the term can carry several meanings, and some definitions may even be codified by law. For example, in the US, digital assets are defined under the American Fiduciary Access to Digital Assets Act and its revised version (hereinafter "RUFADAA").[9] According to Section 2, RUFADAA, digital assets are "*an electronic record in which an individual has a right or interest. The term does not include an underlying asset or liability unless the asset or liability is itself an electronic record.*" Similarly, UNIDROIT recently defined digital assets as "*an electronic record which is capable of being subject to control.*"[10] Therefore, a digital asset can be understood as a sort of electronic record that gives the user certain rights or control. However, the colloquial understanding of digital assets is much broader and does not limit the notion only to those assets that provide the user with certain rights or enable control. This will be further discussed in Chapter 3.

Crucially, the above examples of notions (such as digital assets and virtual property) and their respective definitions describe the very same objects. However, the usage slightly differs depending on the context. To specify what one may imagine under the notion of digital assets, the term "digital assets" should carry a meaning in the broadest sense possible. Accordingly, for the purpose of this book, digital assets are defined as anything existing in cyberspace with which humans interact and which is deemed to be of value, if it comes in a specific form (like an in-game object or Bitcoin). This is, of course, a very vague definition. However, the aim is to cover the broad spectrum of digital intangibles existing in cyberspace that may, according to numerous definitions found in legal literature, be digital assets. So digital assets are cryptoassets, NFTs, all sorts of accounts, objects in videogames or virtual reality, audio or video files as well as all kinds of videogame currencies, and software. As will be discussed in Chapter 3, digital assets are not the digital data behind all of these things. They are also not unspecific raw data. To further clarify, I will use the term "*digital intangibles*" as a general category for anything existing in digital form including data (meaning the data behind the digital assets and/or any digital content without specific form) and the term "*digital assets*" for everything digital excluding data (on a generic level).

Chapter 4 will then explore the legal nature of digital assets under the Czech civil code and focus on three selected digital assets. These will be **AI-generated works, social media accounts and bitcoins**. The reason for this selection is that these three assets may serve as model key examples for a broader category of digital assets. The three examples represent different types of what is colloquially understood as

[9] The revised version can be accessed here: https://www.uniformlaws.org/committees/community-home?CommunityKey=f7237fc4-74c2-4728-81c6-b39a91ecdf22.

[10] UNIDROIT. Principles on Digital Assets and Private Law. [online] 24. 6. 2021 [Accessed 2023-03-03]. Available at: https://www.unidroit.org/wp-content/uploads/2023/04/C.D.-102-6-Principles-on-Digital-Assets-and-Private-Law.pdf, p. 16.

digital assets. At the same time, all of the examples have a very unclear legal framework and could be seen as things that do not have any sort of protection (except for contractual).

Another highly important question is the legal nature of digital assets and thus their legal classification. This can essentially be summarized as the question of digital assets according to the applicable law.

Based on our preliminary definition, digital assets are a wide variety of all sorts of intangible digital objects whose legal nature is connected either to intellectual property law or civil law (namely property rights). Furthermore, certain specific digital assets may be categorized under financial law instruments, such as currency, interests, or securities. Additionally, digital assets are often offered to consumers. Consequently, consumer protection laws may apply to them as well. Finally, in many cases, digital assets may be considered personal data; thus, personal data protection rules will govern some aspects connected to digital assets.

The core issues this work examines is connected to the private law aspects of digital assets and the fact that they do not easily fit into the legal framework of either intellectual property law or property law.[11] For these reasons, it is unclear which legal framework defining rights to digital assets applies.[12] This issue not only leaves users with a certain degree of uncertainty but also leaves space for judicial interpretations. And, of course, it represents an opportunity to examine this topic from an academic point of view. This also means that the focus will be on legal categories such as tangible and intangible things, ownership, property, assets, inheritance, copyrighted works and so on. It is important to emphasize that all the legal categories discussed here may carry different meanings and connotations under different jurisdictions.

1.2 A Primer to The Relevant Legal Framework

Digital assets concern multiple fields of law, such as civil law (mainly property rights, obligations, and inheritance law), intellectual property law, consumer law, data protection law, or financial law. Even within each field a number of issues can be addressed — for example, focusing on civil law, one can deal with every single property right separately, or one can focus on practical aspects such as how the custody of digital assets is determined. Furthermore, multiple studies and soft law instruments are available that may be relevant to the subject of this work.

This book mainly focuses on the private law aspects of digital assets. Specifically, Czech private law will be the primary legal framework with an emphasis on property rights, and within property rights, on ownership. Although this topic has

---

11 PERZANOWSKI, Aaron a Jason M SCHULTZ. *The End of Ownership: Personal Property in the Digital Economy.* Cambridge: The MIT Press, 2016. ISBN 0-262-33596-4, p. 20.

12 Ibid.

strong cross-border elements and it could be argued that Czech law will rarely be applicable in disputes surrounding digital assets, several reasons exist why I have chosen it as a legal framework besides the simple fact that I am a lawyer trained in Czech law.

Firstly, on the most general level, this monograph deals with the topic of property and digital intangibles. But property may mean different things for different groups of people. Philosophers see property differently to lawyers, and lawyers understand property differently to laypersons.[13] But in the end, I will use the notion of property as a legal concept. And it is a fluid legal concept that has gone through many changes, seeking to reflect practical needs in the given times. Moreover, both property rights and the number of objects capable of being subject to property rights were historically affected by the socio-economic reality and never became fully static.[14] Additionally, each jurisdiction has its own legal understanding of property and what may become an object of property rights.[15] Therefore, framing the debate under a specific jurisdiction may be useful in order to identify the exact issues under specific jurisdictions and to propose solutions tailored to the given legal system.

Secondly, Czech law recognizes intangible things. Thus, the Czech understanding of intangible things may serve as a good example for certain lessons learnt for other jurisdictions. Thirdly, the Czech Civil Code was inspired by other European civil codes such as the Austrian or German ones. Which means the findings may be of a more universal use. Finally, even though the jurisdiction is small, Czech law will apply in some cases. And in these cases, it is important to know whether Czech law is fit for the purpose. Moreover, it also appears unlikely that the EU will introduce a unifying tool to resolve this issue given that, for example, the categorization of digital content (which will often overlap with digital assets) according to the Digital Content Directive[16] and the Sale of Goods Directive[17] has been left to the Member States. Thus, even if it would make sense to introduce a uniform way of dealing with intangibles, it may be argued that this could be seen as a violation of the principles of proportionality and subsidiarity, as it would massively affect the civil and intellectual property categorisations of different Member States.

In addition to Czech law, some EU legal instruments will be analysed where relevant to the subject or if they serve as a basis for applicable Czech laws.

---

13 PURTOVA, Nadezhda. *Property Rights in Personal Data: A European Perspective*. Kluwer Law International, 2012. ISBN 978-90-411-3802-6, pp. 59–63.

14 Ibid., p. 64.

15 Ibid., p. 66.

16 Directive (EU) 2019/770 of the European Parliament and of the Council of 20 May 2019 on certain aspects concerning contracts for the supply of digital content and digital services.

17 Directive (EU) 2019/771 of the European Parliament and of the Council of 20 May 2019 on certain aspects concerning contracts for the sale of goods, amending Regulation (EU) 2017/2394 and Directive 2009/22/EC, and repealing Directive 1999/44/EC.

1.2.1 The Czech Civil Code

The first important legal instrument that needs to be introduced is the Czech Civil Code. The Czech Civil Code is fairly new, as it came into force in 2014 and replaced the previous Civil Code from 1964. Although numerous provisions of the Civil Code remained the same in their nature, many new ones were introduced. This means that some of the novelty provisions are still waiting for a proper interpretation by the courts. It also means that in some cases, the legal community is somewhat divided on how the provisions should be interpreted.

One of the greatest changes brought by the new Civil Code is that it adopted a concept of **intangible things** which the previous Code did not recognize. According to Section 489 of the Civil Code, a thing is "*everything different from a person which serves the needs of the people*". Intangible things are then defined as "*rights whose nature allows it and other things without corporeal substance.*"[18] This means that when something intangible is supposed to be categorized as a thing under the Civil Code, it must fulfil the criteria in both of these definitions. It also means that for something to be an object of property rights (i.e. rights *in rem* according to the Civil Code), it must be a thing in the first place. These two primary rules will be central to the classification of digital assets as described in Chapter 4.

A few more legal categories are found under Czech law that require further clarification, as they may be relevant for digital assets. These are **ownership, property and property rights**. Each category may present a language barrier, since different legal jurisdictions may have a different understanding of these concepts. As a result, introductory remarks for these categories under Czech law is required.

Under Czech law, numerous types of property rights / rights *in rem* (*iura in rem*) are found. These include: ownership and co-ownership, possession and various property rights in others' things (*iura in re aliena*).[19] An example of such rights in others' things is right of superficies[20], easements[21] or a pledge/lien.[22] What all of the property rights have in common is that their respective objects must be a thing in the legal sense. Moreover, it is apparent that many such property rights were created for tangible things.

According to Section 1011 of the Civil Code, "*Everything that belongs to someone, all their tangible and intangible things constitute that person's ownership*". In short, ownership is all the tangible and intangible things that a person owns. Following on from this definition, Section 989 adds that a "*person who took a thing to keep it as its owner shall hold the right of ownership.*" It is apparent from the wording that this clause has been designed for the physical world and tangible things. The

[18] Section 496, paragraph 2, Civil Code.

[19] DVOŘÁK, Jan, Jiří ŠVESTKA and Michaela ZUKLÍNOVÁ. *Občanské právo hmotné.* Praha: Wolters Kluwer, 2015. ISBN 978-80-7478-935-9, pp. 24–25.

[20] Section 1240 and following, Civil Code.

[21] Section 1275 and following, Civil Code.

[22] Section 1312 and following, Civil Code.

aforementioned represents just a brief introduction and these concepts naturally represent more than the simple wording found under the Civil Code. However, these definitions should suffice for the purposes of providing the reader an idea of what constitutes ownership under Czech law and how ownership is created.

The Civil Code also recognizes the categories of property and assets. Here, gaining a full understanding is more complex. Under Section 495 of the Civil Code, property is "*the totality of what belongs to a person.*" Furthermore, property is part of one's assets, together with their debts.[23] One may imagine the relationship between these categories as the following:

$$\text{assets} = \text{property} + \text{debts}$$

However, this equation does not provide a complete answer to the question of what exactly property is. Nor does the general definition of "*the totality of what belongs to the person*".

Another legal category is relevant here, namely inheritance, or the so-called "decedent's estate." According to Section 1475, paragraph 2 of the Civil Code, the decedent's estate includes "*the entire assets of a decedent except for the rights and duties exclusively bound to them personally, unless they* [the assets] *have been acknowledged or enforced as a debt before a public body.*" Therefore, whatever represents an asset is also subject to inheritance (unless the rights or duties were purely personal).

Finally, we also find the notion of **matrimonial property** under the Czech Civil Code. Matrimonial property is defined as everything that "*belongs to spouses, has economical value and is not excluded from the legal relations.*"[24] Matrimonial property is thus yet another type of property under Czech civil law for which digital assets may be relevant, as digital assets potentially fall within this category and thus become part of matrimonial property.

The Czech Civil Code also recognizes the category of **digital content** as a result of the transposition of EU directives. The category of digital content is likely the most appropriate category under which digital assets (or digital intangibles in general) can fall under the private law framework. Moreover, as will be further discussed in Chapter 3, understandings of the nature of digital content and digital assets often overlap. In the following paragraphs, I will shortly address the nature of digital content. However, since this book is not about consumer protection, the purpose of this section is merely to demonstrate the difficulty of categorizing something digital and intangible under certain legal systems and to offer another category under which digital assets may fall.

---

[23] Section 495, Civil Code.

[24] Section 708, Civil Code.

The Czech Civil Code does not use the definition of digital content found in EU directives[25], which means that the Code remains silent on the precise definition of digital content. The only clue that the Czech Civil Code provides is that it recognizes digital content contracts as a contract under which "*the provider undertakes to make* ***a thing in digital form*** *(digital content) available to the user for their own use, and the user undertakes to pay a fee for this.*"[26] However, it remains unclear whether "*a thing in digital form*" is the definition of digital content or whether legislators meant a thing in a legal sense. From the Explanatory Memorandum to the Amendment implementing the Digital Content Directive, we can derive the conclusion that legislators indeed consider digital content to be a thing, as the Explanatory Memorandum states that the amendment is built on the assumption that digital content is thing.[27]

Moreover, we can also find the opinion that since the notion carries an EU interpretation, the possible outcome is that legislators basically stated that data produced and supplied in a digital form is a thing in a legal sense under Czech law.[28] This opinion is logical, as if both the Czech and European definitions are combined together, the result is exactly this. The issue is that since the European definition is incredibly broad, we can reach the conclusion that under some circumstances even raw or personal data will be a thing. I find this to be an issue in the original definition more than in the Czech transposition. In the end, it was European legislators who made the category of digital content incredibly broad and defined it through data, which then made its conformity with national laws an obstacle. As a result, digital content is a sort of "stand-alone" category which only applies in the case of consumer rights, and its connection to other private law institutes such as property remains unclear.

Another category relevant for digital assets is the category of **expressions of a personal nature.**[29] The protection of expressions of a personal nature falls under privacy protections. Examples of such expression typically include personal correspondence, text messages, diary entries and other forms of personal communication or one's own notes. Where this category may be relevant in connection to digital assets is social media accounts, emails and similar digital assets which allow for personal communication. Since it is not clear whether digital assets mean the given account itself, what is stored in it, or both (since it cannot be easily separated), considering this category and potential protections via privacy rules is relevant here.

---

25 "*Data which are produced and supplied in digital form*" according to Article 2 paragraph 1 of the Digital Content Directive.

26 Section 2389a, Czech Civil Code.

27 Explanatory Memorandum to the Amendment of the Czech Civil Code. Sněmovní tisk č. 994, p. 84. [online] [Accessed 2023-11-29]. Available at: https://www.psp.cz/sqw/text/orig2.sqw?idd=181044.

28 LIMBERGOVÁ, Zuzana. Směrnice o digitálním obsahu a jejich implementace v právním řádu ČR. *Revue pro právo a technologie*. 2022, vol. 13, no. 25, p. 248.

29 Section 81, paragraph 2, Czech Civil Code.

Finally, in some jurisdictions, digital assets may fall under the category of **securities**.[30] However, Czech civil law generally excludes this option since only a physical deed may be a security with the only exception being book-entry securities.[31] This approach is followed by the Czech National Bank.[32] Digital assets may, however, fall under the purview of financial laws. For those digital assets that are recorded on a digital ledger, we may see laws that specifically create a framework for them. An example of this is the Swiss Distributed Ledger Technology Act.[33] However, financial laws are a separate legal framework which categorizes digital assets differently from civil law. Thus, this topic and the respective categorizations are not relevant to this monograph.

1.2.2 The Copyright Act

As referenced in the introduction, intellectual property is the main source of protections for various digital assets, mostly for in-game objects. Additionally, during early debates on potential legal regimes for virtual worlds, the licensing systems under copyright laws (namely EULAs) were subject to critiques from many authors as will be discussed in Chapter 2. Therefore, the interplay between the Czech Civil Code and the Czech Copyright Act will be a subject of interest in this book.

Under the Copyright Act, a copyrighted work is a "*literary work or any other work of art or a scientific work, which is a unique outcome of the creative activity of the author and is expressed in any objectively perceivable manner including electronic form, permanent or temporary, irrespective of its scope, purpose or significance*."[34] This means that this definition must be fulfilled in order to deem a digital asset a copyrighted work.

The Copyright Act gives authors various moral and economic rights.[35] These rights are what provide various digital assets with legal protections, at least when it comes to virtual worlds, videogames or virtual reality. Such rights are essentially the cornerstone of all the limitations in various licenses and the primary reason why the objects in videogames are not the property of users, but only licenced content.

---

[30] This is the case, for example, in the United States, GOLDBERG, Adam et al. How Are Digital Assets Regulated in the United States and Elsewhere?. *Pillsbury*. [online] 17. 1. 2023 [Accessed 2023-11-29]. Available at: https://www.pillsburylaw.com/en/news-and-insights/digital-assets-regulated-us-elsewhere.html.

[31] Section 514 and following of the Czech civil Code.

[32] Opinion of the Czech National Bank. K možnosti investičních fondů investovat do kryptoaktiv. [online] 19. 5. 2023 [Accessed 2023-11-29]. Available from: https://www.cnb.cz/cs/dohled-financni-trh/legislativni-zakladna/stanoviska-k-regulaci-financniho-trhu/RS2023-05/.

[33] AS 2021 33 Bundesgesetz zur Anpassung des Bundesrechts an Entwicklungen der Technik verteilter elektronischer Register.

[34] Article 2 of the Copyright Act.

[35] Section 2 of Copyright Act.

The relationship between copyrighted works and things under Czech law is not entirely clear. As will be discussed in Chapters 4 and 5, currently no consensus in the legal community is found on whether a copyrighted work fulfils the criteria for an intangible thing. Moreover, no third category exists under Czech law in this respect. Therefore, if something is not a copyrighted work or a thing, no other option can apply under Czech private law with the exception of it being subject to a contract.

1.2.3 Relevant European Legislature

Although European law does not specifically deal with the legal nature of digital assets, nor does it define it as a notion (with the exception of Data Act), some EU legal instruments are nonetheless relevant to the topic. This is mostly as a result of the new EU digital legal framework.

The crucial EU legal instruments to digital assets are the Digital Content Directive and the Sale of Goods Directive. According to both directives, digital content means "*data which are produced and supplied in digital form.*"[36] Such a broad definition means that digital content may in many cases overlap with the notion of digital assets. The Digital Content Directive does not say what digital content is under existing laws (i.e., whether it for instance is a thing or a copyrighted work) and leaves that to the Member States to decide.[37]

A few new EU regulations are also relevant here. The first one is the Data Act. Data Act is a complex piece of legislation that attempts to regulate multiple aspects of both personal and non-personal data. As a result, the regulation contains multiple chapters focusing on different aspects — IoT, B2B data sharing, cloud computing or internation transfers of non-personal data. Data Act also set the data governance as the default model for data sharing instead of data property. Moreover, the Data Act contains a definition and obligations regarding "digital assets" which it sees as a different category than data (and, unfortunately, as a different notion compared to the semantical meaning of digital assets). Moreover, the broad definition of "data"[38] under Data Act includes also what semantically digital assets. And even though the Data Act introduces the data governance as a primary model for data sharing, it does not mean data or digital assets cannot be, at the same time, regulated by national laws' property law.

The topic of digital assets also largely covers the online platforms and service providers. Therefore, the Digital Services Act and Digital Markets Act may be relevant here. In the end, both regulations contain many provision governing platform's

[36] Article 2 Section 1 of Digital Content Directive and Article 2 Section 6 of the Sale of Goods Directive.

[37] Rec. 12 and following of the Digital Content Directive.

[38] According to Art. 2 Data Act data are "*any digital representation of acts, facts or information and any compilation of such acts, facts or information, including in the form of sound, visual or audio-visual recording*".

ecosystems and how they should treat data (which some of may be considered digital assets). Thus, if we look on the topic from a slightly different angle, both DSA and DMA are regulation that governs digital assets.

The dividing line between cryptoassets and digital assets if often blurry. Therefore, another relevant European regulation is MiCA[39]. However, as with all other regulations, MiCA will not give any answers to the proprietary regime of digital assets and only regulates another aspects of the topic.

[39] According to Article 3, Section 2 of the MiCA, cryptoassets are "*a digital representation of value or rights which may be transferred and stored electronically, using distributed ledger technology or similar technology.*"

2 MAPPING THE FIELD OF DIGITAL ASSETS: THE HISTORY OF THE LAW AND DIGITAL INTANGIBLES — REVIEW OF THE LITERATURE

The aim of this chapter is to map existing literature concerning digital assets. Over the years, many authors have studied virtual worlds and other virtual spaces. Such authors often focused on much the same thing — the existence of numerous digital intangibles in cyberspace, and that these digital intangibles exist only in a digital form, are mostly governed by contractual clauses, and that they may represent certain value to their users. Moreover, authors have also focused on how and whether digital intangibles may or may not fit into our current legal system, given their intangible form. In this sense, the purpose of this chapter is to carry out a review of relevant literature and to review and map the current understanding of this field.

2.1 The Fragmentation of Literature

Legal literature dealing with digital intangibles is highly fragmented. Multiple parallel debates can be evidenced concerning this topic across legal literature. The basic overview of such legal literature is as follows:

- **Literature on virtual property.** This literature focuses on legal relationships in the virtual world and introduces the possibility of applying a property law legal framework in virtual objects, as opposed to intellectual property which governs the virtual world. A large part of this literature focuses on user rights in virtual objects subject to restrictions via end-user license agreements (EULAs). Such literature terms virtual objects to be "virtual property".
- **Literature on digital assets.** Here, on the one hand, one can yet again encounter literature dealing with the ownership and transfer of digital objects (only this time called "digital assets"). A significant part of this literature focuses on so-called digital inheritance. At the same time, digital assets are often connected to cryptoassets, thus another body of the literature focuses on the financial law aspects and on ways of using various digital assets as financial instruments. But from a private law perspective, legal literature again frequently focuses on applying a property law regime to digital intangibles.

- **Literature on data and the ownership of data.** Although data is a notion far more abstract than digital assets (as will be argued in Chapter 3), the core argument of the empowerment of data holders and the fostering of a digital economy is increasingly appearing across legal literature on data ownership. Additionally, a significant part of this literature analyses the moral and ethical implications of data ownership, especially the segment of the debate that deals with personal data. But, as in the case of virtual property and digital assets, we yet again find a strain of literature that seeks to identify a suitable existing legal framework to assign rights to a digital intangible.
- **Literature on cryptoassets.** A huge body of literature is also found here that deals with the topic of cryptoassets and their legal nature. Naturally, this body of literature is heavily focused on the financial law aspects and therefore not a core subject of this book. However, some work in this respect is dedicated to the legal nature of cryptoassets according to private law. This means dealing with issues such as whether assets like Bitcoin are an object of ownership and whether individuals can enjoy property rights to these assets.
- **Literature on a shift in property rights.** Finally, publications exist that deal with the future of ownership in a digitalized world and digital economy. This literature does not explicitly mention data, digital assets, cryptoassets or virtual property as its primary subject. The idea behind these works is more that the no property rights apply for digital intangibles, and that the digital world is governed by contracts and licenses. The key publications in this respect are *Owned* by Joshua Fairfield and *The End of Ownership* by Jason Schultz and Aaron Perzanowski.

More subcategories than the above may be found in legal literature; however, the provided examples are intended to cover the core themes addressed over the past two decades in terms of digital intangibles. Upon closer examination of the above, a strong similarity is found among all the identified branches — namely, an argument for the application of traditional property concepts to digital intangibles. This theme may be found across all such subcategories. For this reason, it is important to examine literature concerning more than just digital assets, since the identified arguments may be of the same relevance. Ultimately, various branches of digital intangibles are the subject of all the identified literature — albeit only carrying a different name.

In summary, the following literature review focuses on that selected legal literature dealing with a phenomenon which can otherwise be described as **the impact of digital intangibles on private law**.

2.2 Virtual Property[40]

Although it might appear unusual to begin a book about digital assets with a literature review on virtual property, a very good reason exists for such a methodology. As stated in Chapter 1, the underlying theme of this work is the applicability of current private law on the intangibles existing in cyberspace. And the literature tackling what is termed "virtual property" is exactly about that. In fact, it appears to represent the very first legal literature that sought to capture the shift from the physical world into the virtual one and analyse the legal implications of this change.

The emergence of virtual worlds has led to a discussion of the legal aspects of these worlds. In particular, the discussion revolved around the property relationships that exist in virtual worlds. As a result, many legal scholars began to explore the legal implications of virtual objects with which users interact on a daily basis. The debate covered not only property rights, but also contract law, licensing and intellectual property. At the heart of the debate was whether the rights to virtual objects should be of a proprietary nature and in the hands of users, as opposed to the existing system where everything digital was protected by intellectual property rights and all rights belonged to the company operating the given virtual world. Evidently, such a debate on virtual property was the first to give rise to the idea that traditional property law might serve as a legal framework to assign rights to digital intangibles.

Multiple authors have contributed to the debate concerning rights in virtual worlds. I will not delve into every single article or book written on this topic and instead will only focus on a few selected works. This will mostly be works by law professor Joshua Fairfield, as his article on virtual property[41] is largely credited with sparking the whole debate. I will also look into Lastowka's and Hunter's "The Laws of the Virtual Worlds"[42] which I consider to be the second pivotal work on this topic. Thereafter, I analyse the resultant literature on this subject, including a number of newer works. The question of the nature of virtual property will be specifically examined, as per these articles, including the apparent motives behind the trend of applying an ownership framework to virtual worlds.

The first work I would like to discuss is the "The Laws of the Virtual Worlds". In this work, Lastowka and Hunter conducted a major analysis on how virtual worlds work and how similar they are to the physical world. In their article, three aspects of virtual worlds are emphasized — namely, that property plays a significant role in these worlds, virtual objects have an economic value, and virtual worlds are

---

40 This subchapter is based on the author's previous work on virtual property. Specifically, this literature review is an extension of a literature review in the author's article on virtual property, see SOUKUPOVÁ, Jana. Virtuální vlastnictví: problémy spojené s přechodem do virtuálního prostředí z pohledu práva a kritika dosavadního přístupu. *Právník*, vol. 162, no. 2.

41 FAIRFIELD, Joshua. Virtual Property. *Boston University Law Review.* 2005, vol. 85, no. 4.

42 LASTOWKA, Greg a Dan HUNTER. The Laws of the Virtual Worlds. *California Law Review.* 2004, vol. 92, no. 1.

immaterial and temporal in their nature.[43] All of these three observations were then repeatedly revisited in subsequent literature. The emphasis on economic value is a very common theme, in particular in all subsequent literature concerning digital intangibles.

This article was also one of the first that investigated whether property rights exist in cyberspace.[44] Alas, the authors failed to offer any answers on how property law works in these worlds, except for observing that the scope of the given rights depends on EULAs.[45] Additionally, the authors stress that virtual worlds are only temporal and the services they provide may conceivably ultimately be deleted from existence.[46] This difference in the position of the user and service provider is also often discussed in the literature on this topic. The factual difference in the power of a user and a service provider is an indisputable fact and something that also cannot be easily altered. It is also something that we should take into account when discussing the possibility of applying an ownership framework in this respect. Ownership presumes an absolute control. Accordingly, the one with absolute control here is typically the service provider, not the user. Thus, giving users ownership rights might be slightly against the core *modus operandi* of this institute.[47]

The above-referenced findings do not appear to be especially groundbreaking from today's point of view. The article is also more of a story about virtual worlds than about the law. Indeed, it is hard to see any wider significance of this article beyond the fact that it serves as an illustration of how lawyers addressed the then new phenomenon of cyberspace and virtual space. But in the end, its value mostly lies in the realization that from a legal point of view, little has really changed during the past 20 years.

Focusing on Joshua Fairfield, we see another piece of work based around the idea of property rights in cyberspace. This is well demonstrated by Fairfield's opening words where he asks the provocative question of whether code designed to function as property in the real world should not be regulated and protected as property in the real world.[48] It is important to stress here that Fairfield's work and his idea of the nature of virtual property is based on common law. I will address this again in Chapter 3. But for now, it is necessary to emphasise that that applying Fairfield's definition of virtual property to civil law jurisdictions (which sometimes happens in legal literature) is not a truly viable method since the understanding of property differs widely.

---

[43] This conclusion is derived from the author's previous work, see SOUKUPOVÁ, Jana. Virtuální vlastnictví: problémy spojené s přechodem do virtuálního prostředí z pohledu práva a kritika dosavadního přístupu. *Právník*, vol. 162, no. 2.

[44] LASTOWKA, Greg a Dan HUNTER. The Laws of the Virtual Worlds. *California Law Review*. 2004, vol. 92, no. 1., p. 30–37.

[45] Ibid., p. 72.

[46] Ibid., p. 51–52.

[47] SOUKUPOVÁ, Jana. Virtuální vlastnictví: problémy spojené s přechodem do virtuálního prostředí z pohledu práva a kritika dosavadního přístupu. *Právník*, vol. 162, no. 2, p. 116.

[48] FAIRFIELD, Joshua. Virtual Property. *Boston University Law Review*. 2005, vol. 85, no. 4, p. 1048.

Going back to the article, two things need to be mentioned. Firstly, for Fairfield, the debate on virtual property is about more than just virtual worlds; rather, it is also about the entirely of cyberspace and about a clash between intellectual property rights and property rights.[49] This is demonstrated by his arguments on how EULAs do not give users rights to their virtual property.[50] Secondly, Fairfield focuses on how traditional property may co-exist next to intellectual property.[51] Here, he basically claims that the rights stemming from virtual property do not exclude property rights in the same manner to physical objects.[52] I find this to be the most important argument in the whole article. In cyberspace, intellectual property is the primary framework. Consequently, the possibility of applying both frameworks, and the search for ways in which this could practically be done, would have arguably been a fruitful course for subsequent literature. Unfortunately, such literature (including Fairfield's own works) focused more on trying to overthrow intellectual property concepts than creating a useful symbiosis of the two.

Probably the best way to demonstrate Fairfield's line of thinking is a direct quote from his *The God Paradox* in which he states: "*Game gods thus routinely insist that all digital objects within their world are governed by the law of intellectual property. Gods hope that by eliminating virtual property interests in virtual worlds and insisting on characterizing disputes as ones about intellectual property, they will maintain control.*"[53] This perfectly summarizes the primary issue Fairfield addresses in all of his works. Moreover, it also illustrates the structure of online legal relationships — and thus the state of things with which Fairfield disagrees.

Other Fairfield's works deserve a mention. One is his monography "Owned", which will be the subject of analysis in the next chapter. The other two are his newest additions — "Bitproperty"[54] and "Tokenized: The Law of Non-Fungible Tokens and Unique Digital Property."[55] Both articles are a reaction to newly appearing technologies and a departure from the previous emphasis on virtual worlds. However, his primary focus remains the same, namely pushing for a traditional property law narrative.

In Bitproperty, Fairfield shifts from virtual worlds to the realm of Blockchain and distributed ledgers, which he sees as an opportunity for a change in property theory. The basis for the article are Fairfield's typical remarks that traditional property law did not survive the transition to the online world, since "*online property interests are either intellectual property interests, or strange amalgams of contract, license, and pseudo-property law, such as those that govern users' interests in*

49 Ibid., p. 1050.
50 Ibid., p. 1082–1084.
51 Ibid., p. 1096.
52 Ibid.
53 Ibid., p. 1054.
54 FAIRFIELD, Joshua. Bitproperty. *Southern California Law Review*. 2014, vol. 88, no. 4.
55 FAIRFIELD, Joshua. Tokenized: The Law of Non-Fungible Tokens and Unique Digital Property. *Indiana Law Journal*. 2022, vol. 91, no. 4.

e-books, MP3s, software, or downloaded movies."[56] In this article, however, he suggests overcoming the current state by changing the nature of property law deriving from what he terms "thingness"[57] towards a system in which property law becomes a law of information. By that, he means information about who owns what.[58] Furthermore, he argues that interpreting property law as a law of information allows for extensions of property law into the online environment, and overcoming the issue of digital objects as intangible things.[59] The aim is basically to "*bridge the physicality divide in property law by asserting that property rights are best understood as information and that property systems are ones in which the form of the property as well as the means of its transfer are methods of conveying information.*"[60]

First, Fairfield's newly created theory reacts to the property law system which revolves around tangible things and where property law is a law of things.[61] Accordingly, it makes sense that seeing property more as information about who owns what represents a possibility to overcome the difference between tangible and intangible things. Especially since technological capabilities already exist that could store such information and allow its transfer. As Fairfield notes, different types of confirmations that convey rights such as deeds or certificates are not new to the field of law.[62]

The evident problem with the proposed system is that that it seems to be tailored for blockchain and cryptoassets while leaving other digital intangibles unmentioned. The precise intended subject of the article is also not clear. It is mentioned throughout the text that the system is intended for digital property and smart property. But these notions are not explained anywhere in text. The fact that the article is called "Bitproperty" is even more confusing. It also does not help that Fairfield claims that property is the "*law of data objects.*"[63] What is meant by "data objects" remains, yet again, completely unexplained to the reader.

Moreover, it is also not clear how the idea of property law as information fits into Fairfield's other works. This idea was then repeated in "Owned" where Fairfield again argued that understanding property as information may lead to the creation of an information-based property system.[64] However, it rather appears that the author grasped the newest technology and inconsistently sought to connect it to the old problem of the non-existence of traditional property law online.

That being said, Fairfield is certainly correct that property law is currently a law of things and this "thingness" represents a critical obstacle to introducing property law protections over intangibles. As a result, overcoming this limitation in which

---

56 FAIRFIELD, Joshua. Bitproperty. *Southern California Law Review*. 2014, vol. 88, no. 4, p. 810.
57 Ibid., p. 851.
58 Ibid., p. 811.
59 Ibid., p. 812.
60 Ibid., p. 844.
61 Ibid., p. 849.
62 Ibid., p. 827.
63 Ibid., p. 852.
64 FAIRFIELD, Joshua. *Owned: Property, Privacy, and the New Digital Serfdom*. Cambridge: Cambridge University Press, 2017. Chapter 6.

the object of property rights is only a thing, is not a complete dead-end in terms of solving the issue.

"Tokenized: The Law of Non-Fungible Tokens and Unique Digital Property" is (at the time of publication of this monograph) Fairfield's latest addition to the debate. As the title suggests, the article focuses on the new trend of NFTs and their ability to be a subject of property rights. As Fairfield points out, NFTs are surrounded with the narrative of "owning" digital art, and as opposed to other digital assets, are unique and thus rivalrous.[65] The idea behind the article can be summarized as follows: NFTs are surrounded with a strong ownership narrative; however, in reality the artistry behind NFTs is still dependent on licensing agreements.[66] Therefore, Fairfield calls for the creation of legal analogies that would allow for ownership online[67], otherwise "*NFTs become copyright licensing with extra steps*."[68] He then applies sections regarding the sale of goods under the Uniform Commercial Code to NFTs to create an analogy and push for an ownership narrative.[69] The article also includes typical remarks that contracting and licensing regimes eradicate the possibility of owning anything digital and that the law has failed to react to this in any way.[70]

Firstly, Fairfield is arguably correct that the ownership premise of NFTs is not in line with the reality whereby licensing agreements can actually put restrictions on owners. From a legal perspective, ownership of a token (if the token itself can even be an object of property rights) is not a guarantee that the person who purchased it has any rights whatsoever to what the token represents.

I also concur that owning anything digital is basically impossible due to contractual and licensing restrictions. However, it seems that Fairfield's attempt to push for an ownership narrative ignores the possibility that perhaps a property framework is not possible to apply to digital intangibles (at least not at this point where, as he himself remarks, everything digital is governed by licensing and contracts). Even with NFTs, intellectual property protecting the actual art behind NFTs simply does not allow for anything other than a license. In some jurisdictions (for example the Czech Republic), artworks cannot be transferred. It is legally impossible. So the application of property rights would always hit this limitation in cases where digital assets are protected by intellectual property law.

A notable fact about this article, however, is that Fairfield does not directly contribute to the debate on virtual property (which is a term he uses only once in this article and otherwise talks about digital property), but actually to the debate on digital assets. Throughout the article, Fairfield uses the terms "digital property" and

65 FAIRFIELD, Joshua. Tokenized: The Law of Non-Fungible Tokens and Unique Digital Property. *Indiana Law Journal*. 2022, vol. 91, no. 4, p. 1263.
66 Ibid., p. 1279, 1284.
67 Ibid., p. 1290, 1300.
68 Ibid.
69 Ibid., pp. 1300–1306.
70 Ibid., p. 1285.

"digital assets" in a very synonymous manner. For example, at the beginning of the article he writes about people "*buying digital assets*"[71] or talks about how "*law[s] have failed to develop systems for creating unique digital assets.*"[72] But in other places he uses the notion of digital property, writing that "*digital property can be subject to whatever terms and conditions the seller chooses to impose*"[73] or that "*digital property in games, Kindle eBooks, purchased movies and music, [and] fully bought-and-paid-for software are currently treated exclusively under the law of intellectual property.*"[74] Moreover, at one point, Fairfield suddenly switches to his old terminology when he poses a question of "*What if one wanted to create an aftermarket in virtual property?*"[75] Fairfield also does not explain what any of these terms mean, although it is apparent from the context of the article that at least NFTs and other tokens are deemed to be both digital assets and digital property. The use of terminology is also inconsistent. On the one hand, Fairfield writes about digital property "in" something; but then in his abstract, he equates unique digital property to the "*digital equivalents of rare artworks, collectible trading cards, and other assets that gain value from scarcity.*" So is digital property just a general term for anything digital or is it actual property existing some form? This also remains unclear.

The above is likely just the author's own inconsistency, but it emphasizes the fact that indeed a need exists for terminological unanimity (which will be the aim of Chapter 3), and that the debate on digital assets is just a terminologically transposed debate on virtual property.

It is apparent from Fairfield's work that he disagrees with the current state whereby everything digital is governed by contracts instead of being subject to property rights. He is correct in describing this reality; he is also correct that contracts are limiting to users. However, his works largely overlook platform-based points of view. In the end, platforms seek to protect what they see as their (often intellectual) property as well. In the case of virtual worlds, it was only logical to choose licenses as the appropriate tool. And in the case of other intangibles, which cannot be classified under the law, it makes sense that the result are innominate contracts that give all rights to the platforms. What Fairfield arguably fails to see is that in the end, it does not matter which legal framework is applicable to digital intangibles. This is because platforms would likely usually phrase their contracts and terms of services in a manner where user rights are limited.

Fairfield also overly pushes a strong narrative about the need for traditional property interests and fights for user rights without actually confronting other opinions. This might be the reason why many of his opinions have not resulted in legislative or regulatory action. Yes, Fairfield certainly started the whole "intellectual property

[71] Ibid., p. 1263.
[72] Ibid., p. 1265.
[73] Ibid., p. 1295.
[74] Ibid., p. 1312.
[75] Ibid., p. 1309.

against traditional property in the digital world" debate. He also offered many ideas on how to change the current system. And his attributes of virtual property were certainly adopted by other authors. However, in the end, his works have not made a greater impact when it comes to specific regulatory solutions or interpretations.

The literature review roadmap highlighted two prominent publications that are difficult to place under any category. One is Fairfield's *Owned*.[76] The other is *The End of Ownership* by Perzanowski and Schultz.[77] Since Fairfield's work is linked to virtual property and the surrounding theme in the virtual property debate is tied to ownership in cyberspace, I will briefly discuss the two publications here.

Firstly, both publications are monographies on the topic. Consequently, it is impossible to list every single idea that the authors present. Both of the publications also work as an introduction to the topic, since they offer an overview of the issue through many examples, explain the legal framework and then try to convince readers that ownership as we know it is not compatible with the functioning of the Internet.

Secondly, both publications were published by American authors. This frames both books into the common law system, which is mostly reflected by the authors referencing either US statutes, or basing their arguments on common law property systems. I will therefore not delve into the details of how the common law property system or US intellectual property works in relation to digital intangibles, since this would depart from the scope of this book which is based on Czech law. However, I will still reflect upon the themes and arguments of both books.

Both publications have the underlying theme of the ending of traditional ownership, which is being replaced by an economy of access which runs on licences. In this system, one cannot control anything digital since users simply do not own the respective rights.[78] Both publications also give convincing examples of how today's contracts limit disposition over digital intangibles.

Many more similarities are found. For example, both publications contain a primer to property law. Both books also stress a lack of privacy, autonomy and control as key issues associated with a lack of ownership. Fairfield, for example, focuses heavily on the independence aspect. He argues that ownership is linked to independence and if we have our access to digital objects limited or cut off, we face the loss of this independence. He then gives a more or less convincing example of how access to (undesired) books may be limited.[79]

Perzanowski and Schulz offer one very convincing argument that the end of ownership is of concern. Specifically, they point out that the shift in the economy

[76] FAIRFIELD, Joshua. *Owned: Property, Privacy, and the New Digital Serfdom*. Cambridge: Cambridge University Press, 2017.

[77] PERZANOWSKI, Aaron a Jason M SCHULTZ. *The End of Ownership: Personal Property in the Digital Eaconomy*. Cambridge: The MIT Press, 2016. ISBN 0-262-33596-4.

[78] FAIRFIELD, Joshua. *Owned: Property, Privacy, and the New Digital Serfdom*. Cambridge: Cambridge University Press, 2017, pp. 15–16.

[79] Ibid., Chapter 5 and Chapter 8.

from owning to sharing may lead to a decline in wealth by some societal groups.[80] Moreover, it makes certain groups of people dependent on price fluctuations.[81] Personally, this argument is probably the most convincing one legal literature offers, since it builds on specific structural sociological and economic consequences more than on sympathy with individual users spending money on digital intangibles.

All three authors also appear to concur that the current intellectual property framework is the main culprit for how the Internet presently functions.[82] Therefore, any debate on the topic is ultimately a clash between intellectual property and any other regime that might undermine its dominance online.

Authors can also be found who were not exactly keen on applying the property rights framework to virtual property. Dan Lawrence, for example, wrote an article in which he finds the application of property law (either directly by law or through court interpretation) to virtual property impossible and also unnecessary.[83] His article again narrows down the topic to virtual worlds, here specifically to the massively multiplayer online games (MMOG) environment. Lawrence raises one very important argument, namely that the practices of software developers preclude the introduction of a property law regime.[84] In such an event, the result would be that developers and service providers would be put into difficult positions as the software medium is not built for independent ownership by users.[85] Moreover, virtual worlds do not exist on their own and require software to function.[86] These practical aspects should not be excluded from the debate. The existence of intellectual property protections excludes the possibility of applying traditional property law regimes by default. Moreover, it is logical that software developers and service providers want their "property" to be protected, and thus apply the only available regime (intellectual property). The introduction of traditional property law might, therefore, create chaos whereby it would be unclear which framework applies and for which cases. This will not be the case for all digital assets since not all of them fall under the intellectual property framework. However, for those that do, the practical obstacles of the introduction of a traditional property law regime cannot be overlooked.

80 PERZANOWSKI, Aaron a Jason M SCHULTZ. *The End of Ownership: Personal Property in the Digital Economy.* Cambridge: The MIT Press, 2016. ISBN 0-262-33596-4, p. 170.

81 Ibid., p. 171.

82 FAIRFIELD, Joshua. *Owned: Property, Privacy, and the New Digital Serfdom*. Cambridge: Cambridge University Press, 2017, Chapter 8; PERZANOWSKI, Aaron a Jason M SCHULTZ. *The End of Ownership: Personal Property in the Digital Economy*. Cambridge: The MIT Press, 2016. ISBN 0-262-33596-4, pp. 173–174.

83 LAWRENCE, Dan E. It Really Is Just a Game: The Impracticability of Common Law Property Rights in Virtual Property. *Washburn Law Journal.* 2008, vol. 47, no. 2, p. 507.

84 Ibid., pp. 507, 514.

85 Ibid., p. 514.

86 Ibid., p. 515.

Similarly to Lawrence, Christopher Cifrino was also highly sceptical about the property framework being applied to virtual objects.[87] His main argument can be summarized that EULAs offer the possibility to tailor the law according to the needs of developers and according to the virtual world's functioning.[88] He also sees the introduction of traditional property law to the virtual world as something that might lead to the end of virtual worlds.[89] This argument is not completely erroneous. In the end, every platform is different and having a one-size-fits-all solution is impractical. Cifrino also looks at the issue from the point of view of developers (similarly to Lawrence), which is something often missing in the case of other authors, namely Fairfield.

To move forward to today, three recent additions to the virtual property debate deserve a mention here. In 2020, Kateryna Nekit wrote an article[90] where she deals with the question of whether social media accounts can be an object of virtual property. In her article, Nekit linked the virtual property debate to digital assets when she wrote that a "*virtual property right can be defined as a specific type of ownership, the object of which are digital assets.*"[91]

I find this claim to be problematic for multiple reasons. Virtual property, as explained above, is a term that refers to an object of relationships such as in-game objects. Therefore, it is difficult to understand why the object of the specific type of ownership which Nekit mentions is not the virtual property itself. Especially since in another part of the article virtual property is used as an object.[92] Moreover, Nekit also links digital assets to the attributes of Fairfield's virtual property (i.e., being rivalrous, persistent and interconnected).[93] In short, if a digital asset fulfils these criteria, they may be an object of virtual property rights. On the one hand, this proves that the debates on digital intangibles are indeed interconnected. On the other hand, it creates a considerable confusion, especially since it takes the former theoretical definition of virtual property and applies it to digital assets for the sole purpose of creating some sort of category of ownership which the author calls a "virtual property right."

What is likely the newest addition to the virtual property debate is an article by Xiaochen Mu.[94] The basis of his article is not different from other works on virtual property — virtual property is valuable, it needs to be protected as an investment,

87 CIFRINO, Christopher J. Virtual Property, Virtual Rights: Why Contract Law, Not Property Law, Must Be the Governing Paradigm in the Law of Virtual Worlds. *B.C. L. REV.* 2014, vol. 55, no. 1.

88 Ibid., pp. 263–264.

89 Ibid., p. 264.

90 NEKIT, Kateryna. Social Media Account as an Object of Virtual Property. *Masaryk University Journal of Law and Technology.* 2020, vol. 4, no. 2.

91 Ibid., p. 208.

92 Ibid., p. 209.

93 Ibid.

94 MU, Xiaochen. The challenge of the emergence of virtual property to the traditional legal theory and the corresponding solutions. *European Journal of Law and Technology*. 2023, vol. 14, no. 1.

users are restricted by EULAs and a need exists for an ownership framework to be applied in order to protect users' rights in their virtual property.[95] What is a novelty, however, is Mu's proposal for creating virtual property rights as a *sui generis* system.

The main arguments of the paper are that virtual property has unique characteristics and thus requires a special legal framework rather than a traditional property law regime. Moreover, Mu proposes that contracts should not be the only legal basis for user rights to their virtual property.[96] For this purpose, Mu suggests a virtual property law system based on a layers theory in which virtual property rights are adopted.[97] In this system, three layers of virtual property exist — items users obtained from service providers (the first layer), items containing personal information (the second layer) and items recreated by users (the third layer).[98] Users would have property rights in the first layer and intellectual property rights in the third layer. For the second layer, users would be granted tort rights.[99] Describing digital assets or virtual property through layers is not uncommon. For example, Millard and Michels argue that three distinct layers exist within a digital file (physical, logical and a content layer).[100] Accordingly, if we combine both, layers of individual digital assets can be found within layers of cyberspace in which the digital assets exist. I believe this perfectly illustrates how complex the digital environment is and why it is so difficult to precisely describe what an object is from the perspective of law.

Mu's paper is certainly ambitious in its content and offers some legislative solutions for a long-running problem. However, many issues can be found with the system he is proposing. Firstly, the entire theory is supposed to be built around virtual property in a broader sense, and yet his theory appears to be particularly tailored just for virtual worlds. It seems questionable that the same layer theory could be applied, for example, to cryptoassets, since they do not have the layers of user content. Similarly, it is unclear how the proposed framework would work together with data and the data economy. Additionally, an entire second layer based on personal information seems to be against personal data protection principles and also somewhat redundant.

On the other hand, a system which recognizes and differentiates the layers of an account and of the content stored in that account is certainly overcoming some of the theoretical issues connected to this topic.

What is missing from Mu's articles is a link to other examples defining virtual property, especially when technology has come a long way since the days of virtual

95 Ibid.
96 Ibid.
97 Ibid.
98 Ibid.
99 Ibid.
100 MICHELS, Johan David a MILLARD, Christopher. The New Things: Property Rights in Digital Files?. *Cambridge Law Journal.* 2022, vol. 81, no. 2.

worlds. Mu's legislative proposal seeks to cover a broad scope of objects that may be virtual property; however, in the end they are only tailored to virtual worlds.

So what can we learn from the strain of literature focusing on virtual property and virtual worlds? The discourse surrounding virtual property initially emerged as part of a broader discussion concerning users' rights, or the lack thereof, within virtual worlds. Central to this still ongoing debate has been the interplay between traditional property and intellectual property, as no alternative framework has adequately addressed the complexities of users' rights in virtual objects. The debate also had very strong common law associations, since many of the authors who contributed to the debate were from common law jurisdictions.

Over time, the usage of the term "virtual property" has declined (although contemporary scholarly pieces on this topic can still be found, such as Nekit's article from 2020[101], or Mu's article from 2023[102]). What has not declined, however, is the idea behind the body of legal literature that private law as we understand it was built for the physical world and that the current system that heavily inclines towards intellectual property might not be suitable for the digital economy of today. The following section will compare two crucial publications on this topic released during the past two years, which illustrate how these problematic aspects (and laws themselves) have not evolved in this respect since the start of the 2000s.

2.3 Digital Assets

It is hard to determine when exactly legal literature on virtual property declined and literature on digital assets emerged. Especially since both notions have appeared in literature since the 1990s and early 2000s.[103] However, it appears that the time virtual worlds lost their appeal and the era of social media and blockchain arose represented a defining moment that saw the concurrent rise of literature on digital assets (and especially cryptoassets).

A literature review on digital assets could take many routes, since the topic covers not only private law aspects, but also financial law aspects. However, for the purposes of this work the subsequent paragraphs will focus solely on the private law aspects of digital assets. More precisely, it will focus on literature dealing with

101 NEKIT, Kateryna. Social Media Account as an Object of Virtual Property. *Masaryk University Journal of Law and Technology*. 2020, vol. 4, no. 2.

102 MU, Xiaochen. The challenge of the emergence of virtual property to the traditional legal theory and the corresponding solutions. European Journal of Law and Technology. 2023, vol. 14, no. 1.

103 For example, ZORICH, Diane. *Introduction to Managing Digital Assets: Options for Cultural and Educational Organizations*. Oxford: Oxford University Press, 1999. ISBN 978-0892365463; STEPHENS, Molly. Sales of In-Game Assets: An Illustration of the Continuing Failure of Intellectual Property Law to Protect Digital-Content Creators. *Texas Law Review*. 2002, vol. 80, no. 6.; CASTRONOVA, Edward. Virtual Worlds: A First-Hand Account of Market and Society on the Cyberian Frontier. CESifo Working Paper. 2001, (618).

either property rights in digital assets (including cryptoassets) and on literature focusing on fiduciary access to digital assets. Ultimately, the issue of inheriting digital assets prompted this body of literature and even led to the adoption of RUFADAA in the US.

Literature on the inheritance of digital assets is often practically oriented and focuses on how contracts with service/platform providers limit the possibility of inheriting digital assets.[104] The conclusions are typically that digital assets are not user property and that a lack of clarity exists in existing legislation regarding inheritance options.[105] Consequently, it is contracts and terms of service that stipulate which entity owns what and how digital assets are transferred.[106]

Natalie Banta has written two more or less similar pieces on digital assets. Both articles focus on the application (or lack thereof) of traditional property law and inheritance law on digital assets.

In "Inherit the Cloud: the Role of Private Contracts in Distributing or Deleting Digital Assets at Death" Banta argues that contractual clauses limiting the transfer of digital assets after death are in violation of succession laws and should be void.[107] Banta does not define what digital assets are, but she gives plenty of examples, such as online accounts, domain names, documents, books and videos in digital form.[108] So we may observe that the article belongs to the larger group of literature focused on digital intangibles. Although the article is based on US succession law, some arguments, thoughts and observations are still useful for a more general debate.

Crucially, although Banta focuses on inheritance aspects, her article in many ways resembles the literature on virtual property. For example, she points out the differences in control over tangible and intangible assets[109] and observes that the digital assets are mostly regulated by a private contract between a company and an individual.[110] She also mentions the monetary value of digital assets[111]. This is accompanied by stressing the emotional value of certain digital assets.[112] The aspect of emotional value and focus on digital assets replacing personal tangible things such as letters, scrapbooks or photographs is an interesting observation, which brings a new argument to the debate. Many papers focus solely on monetary value — users pay for digital assets and do not have any rights in return. But the perspective that

[104] MCCARTHY, Laura. Digital Assets and Intestacy. *Boston University Journal of Science and Technology Law*. 2015, vol. 21, no. 2; HOPKINS, Jamie. Afterlife in the Cloud: Managing a Digital Estate. *Hastings Science & Technology Law Journal*. 2013, vol. 5, no. 2.

[105] MCCARTHY, Laura. Digital Assets and Intestacy. *Boston University Journal of Science and Technology Law*. 2015, vol. 21, no. 2, pp. 386–387.

[106] Ibid., p. 390.

[107] BANTA, Natalie. Inherit the Cloud: The Role of Private Contracts in Distributing or Deleting Digital Assets at Death. *Fordham Law Review*, vol. 83, no. 2, p. 803.

[108] Ibid., p. 801.

[109] Ibid., p. 802.

[110] Ibid., pp. 801–802.

[111] Ibid., pp. 813–816.

[112] Ibid.

these rights might be desired because one has an emotional attachment to certain digital assets is similarly an important argument (albeit more regulatory than legal).

Accordingly, the primary problem of a lack of control (which in this case is represented by the lack of possible inheritance) in digital intangibles is yet again being discussed. The difference is only that Banta does not argue to apply the whole property law framework to digital assets. Her primary focus are the limitations after death and possible regulatory changes regarding inheritance. She even notes that the classification of digital assets as property does not automatically mean they are inheritable.[113] Banta also adds that this classification is not important to public policy questions concerning whether contracts may prohibit inheritance.[114] Here we can see how conceptual and regulatory questions may overlap, which leads to incomplete conclusions. Whether digital assets are property or if they can be inherited will depend on each jurisdiction and its understanding of these concepts and how they are interconnected. Classification will presently always be a conceptual question. But it appears that Banta is skipping a conceptual analysis and only argues on a regulatory level. Still, even if the arguments are more regulatory than conceptual, legislators should still be searching for ways to amend laws in a systematic matter and not skip conceptual questions and solely focus on contractual limitations when it comes to inheriting digital assets.

In the second article, Banta analyses how contracts and terms and conditions allocate property rights in digital assets. Her findings, based on evaluating multiple platform terms and conditions, reveal that users often retain property rights to content they submit; however, when it comes to digital assets such as music or videos, they are only provided with licenses.[115] This in itself is not a revolutionary finding. In the end, it makes sense that when it comes to digital assets which are considered intellectual property that an intellectual property regime will apply. What is more interesting is Banta's argument that "*contracts should not be controlling*"[116] and that they "*cannot rewrite the entire system of property for digital assets*."[117] This is her starting point to argue about whether the property concept applies for digital assets. Banta also recognizes that property is a right in *things.*[118] That is something Fairfield sought to overcome in an article referenced in the previous chapter. "Thingness" is still the basis for traditional property law. Alas, Banta does not delve into whether digital assets are things. Instead, she analyses whether any incidents of property apply — i.e., if any bundle of rights is found that might be assigned to digital assets.[119] The outcome of this analysis is that users have some property interests in

[113] Ibid., p. 826.
[114] Ibid., p. 827.
[115] BANTA, Natalie. Property Interests in Digital Assets: The Rise of Digital Feudalism. *Cardozo Law Review*. 2016, vol. 38, no. 3.
[116] Ibid., p. 1107.
[117] Ibid.
[118] Ibid., p. 1108.
[119] Ibid.

digital assets during their life and, therefore, they decide what happens with them after death.[120]

Similarly to Banta, Hopkins wrote an article in which he conceptually analysed the inheritance of digital assets.[121] Hopkins notes that in order to figure out what legal mechanism applies to digital assets upon death, three preliminary questions must be solved — where the digital assets are located, who owns the digital assets, and whether the deceased prepared for a transfer upon death.[122] The first and the last questions are not central to this book. However, the question of ownership of digital assets is crucial, since one must first own something in order to bequeath it upon death. And as Hopkins notes, the ownership of digital assets is typically limited by contracts.[123] This finding itself is not surprising. However, Hopkins' article demonstrates that the question of ownership of digital assets is preliminary to the possibility of their subsequent inheritance. This line of reasoning is something I am going to present in Chapter 4 where I focus on Czech private law and where I also reach the conclusion that without a clear answer as to who owns digital assets, all subsequent issues (like their inheritance) cannot be solved.

Lehavi writes about data and digital assets as objects of property rights.[124] This is a familiar theme repeated many times within legal literature on digital intangibles. Lehavi also notes the typical factual basis behind this topic — digital assets are controlled by contracts and such contracts limit user possibilities such as resale or inheritance.[125] Since Lehavi's focus is mostly on the cross-border aspects of the whole topic, I will only reference a few ideas that might be useful for this book that concern property.

Firstly, Lehavi draws a distinction between data and digital assets.[126] I will focus more on this aspect in the following chapter; but for now, it is important to stress that the author treats the two as different phenomena. Additionally, his work is based on Fairfield, Banta and van Erp — authors who focus on digital intangibles, only terming them either "virtual property", "digital assets" or "data." This gives us a strong indication of only one true debate on digital intangibles, with the only difference between data (in the abstract sense) and digital assets/virtual property being that digital assets are just specific data.

Secondly, Lehavi emphasizes that both data and digital assets require a contextual analysis, since many different types of both data and digital assets are found which may fall under different legal frameworks.[127] This case-by-case approach is

---

[120] Ibid., p. 1120.

[121] HOPKINS, Jamie. Afterlife in the Cloud: Managing a Digital Estate. *Hastings Science & Technology Law Journal.* 2013, vol. 5, no. 2.

[122] Ibid., p. 222.

[123] Ibid., p. 224.

[124] LEHAVI, Amnon. Intellectual Property, Data, and Digital Assets. In: LEHAVI, Amnon. *Property Law in a Globalizing World.* Cambridge University Press, 2019. ISBN 9781108595391.

[125] Ibid., pp. 201–202.

[126] Ibid., p. 200.

[127] Ibid.

logical given the broad array of digital assets. Lehavi then goes through global case law that has dealt with specific digital assets being seen as a property and concludes that no consolidated theory or case law deals with the issue on a general level.[128] This is where his work ends. Lehavi does not delve into a greater conceptual analysis of data or digital under any legal framework. He also does not question whether a property law regime is suitable to apply to digital assets (and data).

His work basically ends with delineating the applicable problems.

On a different note from inheritance, conceptual questions still surround digital assets and their legal nature. As demonstrated, the main conclusion from literature is that digital assets do not have a clear legal nature and placing them within the existing legal framework is simple. Addressing this, Allen writes that three options exist to deal with digital intangibles that cannot be precisely placed within the existing legal framework.[129] We can either deny that they are legally cognizable, put them into some existing legal category, or reform the law so they fit.[130] He then proceeds to advocate for the third option, seeing it as an opportunity to incorporate digital intangibles (or in his case, digital coins) into private law and to make them future-proof.[131] Allen evidently chooses this option because of a lack of certainty that the objects would fit into the existing categories — with which I concur. The two-decades-long debate on this topic is proof that legal analogies do not always work and no certainty exists that they will be adopted by the courts.

2.4 Literature Concerning Data Ownership

Data ownership and distribution rights in data are major topics in the current digital economy. The American Law Institute and European Law Institute (ALI-ELI), for example, has created the Principle for Data Economy[132] that focuses on data transactions and data rights and whose aim is to create a coherent legal data framework for tradeable data.[133] Furthermore, similarly to digital assets and/or virtual property, the lingering question is how to categorize and define data under the law.[134] Moreover, legal scholars have also focused on a process called "commodification of data" in

---

128 Ibid., p. 204.

129 ALLEN, Jason. Property in Digital Coins. *European Property Law Journal.* 2019, vol. 8, no. 1, p. 76.

130 Ibid.

131 Ibid.

132 ALI-ELI. Principles for a Data Economy. [online] 2021. [Accessed 2023-05-22]. Available at: https://www.europeanlawinstitute.eu/fileadmin/user_upload/p_eli/Publications/ALI-ELI_Principles_for_a_Data_Economy_Final_Council_Draft.pdf.

133 Ibid. For more information about the aim, read Principle 1: Purpose of These Principles, p. 14.

134 More on this for example ERP, Sjef van and SWINNEN, Koen, 2022, The legal status of co-generated data. *Technology and Regulation.* 13 June 2022. Vol. 2022, pp. 61–70.

which data is used as a valuable asset and commodity.[135] Currently, data are subject to, and thus controlled under, a "de facto ownership" principle.[136] However, this control over data does not stem from any existing property right, but rather from the factual state and contractual clauses.[137] The dominant view is that data cannot be owned.[138] The current state of how control over data is exercised is not different from how control over digital assets or virtual property is managed. For that reason, a study of existing literature dealing with data ownership may provide some insight into the problem from a slightly different perspective. However, it must be noted that this monograph is not about data; it is about digital assets, which is to some degree a different phenomenon as will be argued in the following chapter. For these reasons, I will only make a few remarks regarding legal literature on this topic in the areas where I believe the topics overlap.

One article which I find particularly useful for the debate is by Koen Swinnen, on the ownership of data.[139] In it, Swinnen offers four recommendations on future research concerning data ownership. These recommendations, however, go beyond the debate on data and can be applied to the digital assets debate as well. As a first recommendation, Swinnen addresses the ownership debate in general. His point is that although legal literature focuses on data ownership, the nature of this ownership is not always clear. Sometimes, this means property law ownership, other times intellectual property or even certain *sui generis* rights to data.[140] This recommendation may also be applied to the debate on digital assets/virtual property, since it revolves heavily around ownership — but it is often unclear what kind of ownership is meant or for which jurisdictions.

Swinnen also points out that basically three ownership regimes exist — property law ownership, intellectual property and some kind of *sui generis* right.[141] The same three regimes also apply to digital assets.

As his second recommendation, Swinnen notes that it is important to be precise when defining the object of ownership.[142] Although his point is mostly about the distinction between data, information, or data files[143], he makes an important distinction between data that cannot be owned because of its nature and data that is more specific, and for which ownership is not completely impossible.[144] Swinnen

[135] SWINNEN, Koen. Ownership of Data: Four Recommendations for Future Research. *Journal of Law, Property, and Society*, vol. 5, no. 3, p. 143.
[136] Ibid., p. 143–44.
[137] Ibid., p. 144.
[138] Ibid., p. 141.; HUMMEL, Patrik, Matthias BRAUN a Peter DABROCK. Own Data? Ethical Reflections on Data Ownership. *Philosophy & Technology*. 2021, vol. 34, no. 3.
[139] SWINNEN, Koen. Ownership of Data: Four Recommendations for Future Research. *Journal of Law, Property, and Society*, vol. 5, no. 3, p. 144.
[140] Ibid., pp. 146–148.
[141] Ibid, p. 148.
[142] Ibid., p. 154.
[143] Ibid., pp. 154–55.
[144] Ibid., pp. 154–160.

concludes that not all data follows the same regime.[145] This case-by-case approach is exactly something which should be followed in the case of digital assets. For example, both in-game objects and social media accounts are considered to be digital assets. However, as legal objects, both significantly differ. The legal nature of one is often a copyrighted work and the legal nature of another may be unclear. So a one-size-fits-all solution is not possible with such intangibles, at least not according to current laws.

Swinnen makes two more recommendations. One is that lawyers should be cooperating with IT specialists in order to specify the objects of ownership.[146] The other is to include more possible stakeholders into the debate than just data producers, data users and data subjects.[147] Specifically, creditors are often overlooked in the debate even though data might be valuable to them in cases where they seek to either access it as an asset or to sell it.[148] Both recommendations again also fit digital assets. Determining the object of ownership together with IT specialists is a recommendation that is likely applicable to any related aspect regarding IT law. Moreover, similarly to data, digital assets might be of considerable importance to creditors, especially if the digital assets in question are cryptoassets.

To conclude, Swinnen's four recommendations adding to the literature on data ownership are also applicable to the debate on digital assets. In the end, the underlying questions concerning the legal framework for digital intangibles are the same and the applicability of this article only stresses that the two issues cannot be completely separated.

An argument is also raised by Swinnen that for the purposes of property law, data must be specified, i.e., captured on a medium such a case-file.[149]

Similarly to Swinnen's article, a work by Hummel, Braun and Dabrock addresses several issues that may fill a number of gaps in the debate on digital intangibles.[150] The article maps the current discourse regarding data ownership with one clear finding — the discourse is fragmented even among those who actually advocate for data ownership. The authors do not define data. But it is apparent from the text that they treat it as a broad category which also includes what previous literature termed "virtual property".[151] The article actually connects the debate on virtual property to the debate on data ownership.[152] However, this link serves only to distinguish the problems inherent in the fact that some intangibles are rivalrous and, therefore,

[145] Ibid., p. 160.
[146] Ibid., p. 165.
[147] Ibid., p. 167.
[148] Ibid., pp. 170–71.
[149] ERP, Sjef van and SWINNEN, Koen, 2022, The Legal Status of Co-generated Data. *Technology and Regulation*. 13 June 2022. Vol. 2022, p. 64.
[150] HUMMEL, Patrik, Matthias BRAUN a Peter DABROCK. Own Data? Ethical Reflections on Data Ownership. *Philosophy & Technology*. 2021, vol. 34, no. 3.
[151] Ibid., p. 550.
[152] Ibid.

require a legal framework separate from intellectual property.[153] Still, this serves as further proof that the debate on data ownership is part of the debate on digital assets/virtual property and whatever else digital intangibles might be called.

Another important observation made by Humme, Braun and Dabrock is that contract law does not solve the question who owns data, nor does it establish it.[154] Although intellectual property assigns ownership in intangibles, it only applies if the act of creation applies. Which is not the case with data.[155] This means that although contract law is a useful tool for legal relationships where data is present, it is not built on any clear conceptual legal basis. It also means the question of ownership is left open for the law to establish and the intellectual property framework is not the one that can be applied here.

The article also provides multiple sceptical viewpoints regarding data ownership, which may also apply to digital assets.[156] Firstly, when possessing data, no sole possessor and exclusive users are found since data can be duplicated. Secondly, the exclusion of other users is almost impossible. Therefore, the ownership of data is not the correct applicable category and access to data should apply as a concept instead.[157] Thirdly, intellectual property (if it can be considered property) cannot be the right framework, since data is not created or invented.[158] The last point will not apply to many digital assets which actually fall under the intellectual property law framework (such as in-game objects). However, for other digital intangibles such as cryptoassets (and, of course, data), intellectual property is simply not the right framework either. Similarly, one must agree that applying a traditional property law framework may be a bit of a stretch.

Similarly to Swinnen, the authors propose three possible solutions — traditional property, *sui generis* rights, and a quasi-property concept.[159] The solution proposed is to shift from the traditional meaning of ownership to some sort of quasi-ownership concept based on control.[160] The authors see this as a solution, since ownership and property terminology would be abandoned and the law would solely focus on a selected bundle of rights that may be useful for data control.[161] This is a possible solution and may go beyond just data. In the end, digital assets may benefit from a system of quasi-property as well. The issue is what should follow — could this be a basis for new regulation? Or can current laws be interpreted only to the extent of allowing for some rights resembling ownership and not for others?

153 Ibid.
154 Ibid., p. 548.
155 Ibid., p. 548.
156 Ibid., p. 549.
157 Ibid., p. 549.
158 Ibid.
159 Ibid., p. 552.
160 Ibid., p. 554.
161 Ibid.

Finally, an interesting intersection is evidenced in data literature and digital asset concepts, focusing on issues with a *numerus clausus* of property rights and objects. Specifically, this is found in an article by Sjef van Erp.[162] Firstly, the title of the given article suggests it deals with data; however, the scope is somewhat stricter. Indeed, the author emphasizes that many different notions exist under which we can encounter digital objects in cyberspace — i.e., virtual property, data and digital assets.[163] He then narrows down the subject of his article to data which "can be specified" and have economic value.[164] This approach is understandable, since it makes the application of the law much easier for a specific subject. However, I still find it too confusing to call everything "data", only to narrow it down to specific data. I believe an approach which would either choose virtual property or digital assets might be more fitting than calling everything "data". This is also what makes the terminological approach in this book different from van Erp's article, even though I concur with the requirement of specificity.

Secondly, and more importantly, van Erp notes that property law has a very strict approach towards what may be the object of these rights. As a result, data, even specific data, cannot fulfil these requirements.[165] He also stresses that some civil jurisdictions do not even recognize intangible things, which makes the application of property rights much more complicated.[166] Unfortunately, the article does not go deeper into an analysis of property rights. This makes sense, however, since the focus is on the object of these rights and not on the actual rights *in rem*.

Thirdly, the article briefly mentions the concept of control and asks whether we should use it instead of possession, since possession is linked to physical form.[167] Unfortunately, the author does not offer any answer. In the end, he admits that such questions surrounding data are presently unanswerable.[168] However, this itself serves as the perfect basis for future research. The issues with data (or digital assets, or whatever terms we use) and traditional property have been clearly outlined and identified. Thus, we may start to build upon them and address the respective issues.

It is clear that data is crucial to the digital economy and an interest exists in creating a system that fosters data flows. However, this needs to be separated from the issue of digital assets. Digital assets can likely be considered as data (in the sense that almost everything can be considered data) and digital assets consist of data. Indeed, both issues — the property rights to data and digital assets — have the same core arguments. Moreover, both are connected to access and control and sharing. Despite this, they are still two are separate legal avenues and should be treated as such.

---

[162] ERP, Sjef van. Ownership of Data: The Numerus Clausus of Legal Objects. *Brigham-Kanner Property Rights Conference Journal.* 2017, volume 6. Revised and expanded version.

[163] Ibid., pp. 243–244.

[164] Ibid.

[165] Ibid., pp. 235–241.

[166] Ibid., p. 241.

[167] Ibid., pp. 251–252.

[168] Ibid., pp. 254–257.

2.5 Identified Gaps

Even by limiting the focus solely to the private law aspects of digital intangibles, the number of issues associated with the topic remains broad. That said, the underlying issues remain the same — a group of digital intangibles, such as data, cryptoassets, in-game objects and many others under different names, is found whose legal nature remains unclear and subject to challenge. These digital intangibles are typically protected by contracts and/or licences, which limit any disposition with them. Moreover, without specifically tailored contracts the legal protections given to some digital intangibles would either remain ambiguous or non-existent, as current laws often do not grant them any protections. Legal literature, therefore, has often challenged the existing legal framework surrounding digital intangibles, seeking to come up with analogies to the existing traditional property law framework, or seeking new regulatory solutions. Such literature also often revolved around common law property systems or addressed the issue on a more theoretical level.

Multiple legal problems can be identified from the above-analysed literature. Firstly, this literature contains a vast spectrum of digital intangibles ranging from in-game objects, through to cryptoassets, to data. I also see a pattern that every time a new technology appears (such as cryptoassets, or becomes more relevant to the economy (like data, legal literature reacts and a new body of work appears. However, little to no research is evident into whether all such studies of digital intangibles should be placed under the same category. Superficially, it makes sense to include everything digital into one umbrella term. On the other hand, are there not simply too many differences across individual digital intangibles? For example, are not some parts "code" and others just different assets on a server? Are they not created in the same manner? Do they have the same value and function to users and service providers? And how to draw a line? This will be explored and addressed in greater detail in Chapter 3.

Secondly, the issue multi-layered, including concerning how the law should actually regulate and offer protections. An underlying layer of code, bytes and data is evident. This is followed by a layer of accounts, which grants access to all these intangibles. And finally, there is a layer with whatever the account gives us access to, such as specific in-game objects or anything stored on that account. This complex architecture appears highly challenging for the current legal framework to comprehend.

A large empirical gap in research is also evident. By empirical, I mean a lack of data or research into whether the current legislative framework is effective, whether it fulfils its goals, or even whether society prefers traditional ownership to access or does not actually care.

Furthermore, a large number of practical technological aspects appear to be the reason why contract law is deemed the primary solution for the inherent legal issues. Especially in cases where the object of a legal relationship is not protected by intellectual property laws and thus may be deprived of legal protections at all.

Finally, it is apparent that those issues outlined more than 20 years ago still persist. Although many authors sought to push the traditional property law narrative, it was never really adopted — neither on a regulatory level nor a conceptual one. No consensus can even be found on whether the issue should be tackled on a conceptual level at which property law analogies are applicable, or whether ta new *sui generis* system adopted by the policymakers should be used. It is also uncertain whether digital intangibles could be considered a thing, and if so, whether it would be tangible or intangible. The result is that we have ended up with a plethora of theories, notions and proposals — but no action. Additionally, it also appears that no matter which legal framework is applied, as long contract law is deemed applicable, developers/service providers see no reason to grant users any rights to digital intangibles. Accordingly, we may just go from licence to lease.

Based on legal literature, the debate on digital intangibles may develop in two ways. The problem may be tackled on the most general level on which data and digital assets would be treated as the same thing. This would mean that the legal framework for both would be the object of research. The second possibility is to separate digital assets from data. This makes the debate slightly easier, since digital assets are more specific as an object of research; thus finding an applicable framework and testing its limits might be more precise. In this monograph, as is evident from the research questions, I will follow the second path and focus on digital assets as a specific form of data.

It is also apparent that many gaps still exist in this field — but this book aims to fill only some. Firstly, no works have properly addressed grey areas under Czech law. Property and property rights vary across jurisdictions, so taking a specific legal system and applying it to specific digital assets is something that may be helpful in this debate, because the examined area will be narrowed down to specific legal rules. The precise identification of unanswered aspects within a particular legal system could prove beneficial for any future regulatory measures. The premise stemming from available legal literature is that for many digital intangibles, no specific protections exist under the law or that their application is highly uncertain.

Secondly, many different notions are found for the topic. The issue of terminological confusion was already raised by Pałka[169] regarding the notion of virtual property. However, his analysis stopped at the virtual property debate and did not go further. Therefore, space exists for an analysis of differing existing notions (be it digital assets, data, virtual property or cryptoassets) which could unify usage in the future and prevent more confusion. Moreover, a clear distinction should be made between digital assets and data, since the debate on whether one or the other can be owned is ongoing for both.

Thirdly, space exists for evaluation of what "control" may mean under the law. Can it be analogically used for possession? Or does it require a new system to

[169] See PAŁKA, Przemysław. *Virtual Property — Towards a General Theory*. 2017, p. 104–107.

emerge? Is ownership really the only solution as legal literature implies? This is another area that remains unanswered.

Finally, the evident overreaching issue with digital assets is that with no clear single legal framework we are left with multiple legal frameworks that may potentially apply. In the end, it is at the discretion of those persons applying the law (which most often will be a judge) as to which possible legal framework they will choose, and towards which interpretation they will incline. This, however, represents massive legal uncertainty. It also underscores that whichever interpretation a judge comes across and rules on will determine the results. For example, whether traditional property law applies or the protection of privacy prevails. Consequently, the primary legal issue surrounding digital assets (or all digital intangibles) is that with no unifying interpretation and ambiguous legal rules, we are unable to determine how the law protects any of these, nor which respective rights subjects enjoy.

3 AN ANALYSIS OF THE NOTION OF DIGITAL ASSETS: A TERMINOLOGICAL CONUNDRUM[170]

The previous chapter demonstrated how legal literature concerning the law and various digital objects and other digital phenomena is somewhat fragmented. As a result, many different notions are used across legal (and in some cases non-legal) literature such as virtual property, virtual assets, digital assets, res digitales, data, cryptoassets, or smart property. Similarly, the notions used in specific legal instruments differ. But are those notions essentially the same or do they differ? Is their use connected to a specific context, or can it be more universal? And is the existence of a single umbrella concept helpful to the law and legal literature, or does it actually make the application of the law more complicated?

The aim of this chapter is to analyse the differing notions that have appeared in the past two decades across legal literature with an emphasis on the notion of digital assets. The first part of this chapter deals with similar notions and analyses what these notions have in common and how they differ. The second part then specifically focuses on the notion of digital assets, its origin in legal literature and legal instruments, and compares this notion to the other notions analysed in the first part. Studying the various definitions of digital assets should provide an answer to the question of the nature of digital assets and how understandings may differ depending on the context.

An attempt at a clarification of terminology is not entirely without merit. Indeed, digital assets are a notion appearing in connection with multiple legal fields such as financial law, civil law or intellectual property law. In all these legal fields, questions of the nature of digital assets under the law, or whether new regulations are required, are common. But in the end, digital assets are usually not a codified notion (as opposed, e.g., to digital content). **This means that the first step for categorization under any legal field is to have a clear understanding of its respective nature.** What I will argue is that an understanding of the meaning of each notion and where they overlap is **crucial for both the regulatory and conceptual debates** that often surround the topic. If a suitable legal regime is to be either applied or

[170] A shortened version of this chapter was published in the Lawyer Quarterly, see SOUKUPOVÁ, Jana. Analysis of the Notion of Digital Assets in the Context of Fragmented Terminology. *The Lawyer Quarterly*. 2024, vol. 14, no. 3.

created for all sorts of digital intangibles, it is first important to understand what such a debate is to be about. Moreover, a clarification of the terminology may help legislators to avoid overlapping regulatory proposals. We presently see frequent calls for the regulation of either digital assets, digital inheritance, data, cryptoassets and so on. This fragmentation leaves legislators in a tough position, needing to first decipher what all these notions mean and how they are related to each other while avoiding unnecessary regulation.

3.1 A Roadmap for the Notion

As the literature review indicated, a host of legal literature, legal documents, and legal instruments are focused on something that could be described as digital intangibles. However, these intangibles come under many different names. Therefore, the lingering question is — are all these notions essentially describing the same phenomenon? To find an answer to this, it is important to first evaluate the meaning behind all these terms.

Generally, the notions can be sorted into three categories:

- First, we have notions originating/existing solely in legal literature. These are terms whose origin is entirely rooted in legal literature and that do not appear to be used in other fields or in legal norms.
- Second, there are many notions originally existing outside of the law which found their way into legal literature. This is a classic case of trying to apply law to phenomena existing outside of it.
- Finally, there are notions that have already been codified. These notions have a definition directly in the law and carry the meaning ascribed to them by legislators. These notions therefore primarily carry a meaning defined by the law.

Naturally, some notions will fit into more than one category. For example, the notion of digital assets may be found both outside of legal terminology, as well as in many legal documents, and in some countries even within the law itself.[171] This will mostly depend on the given jurisdiction. Such simplification will help us to navigate the first part of the analysis. The following chapters will examine the three defined categories.

3.1.1 Notion Originating from Legal Literature

Based on the findings from the previous chapter, four notions appear to have originated solely from legal literature. The four notions are (i) virtual property, (ii) smart

[171] Which is the case with the Revised Uniform Fiduciary Access to Digital Assets Act.

property, (iii) digital property, and (iv) res digitales. There are likely dozens of other notions coined by legal scholars over the past two decades; however, the four here are the ones that I have specifically identified while conducting the literature review. It also should be pointed out that three of these terms (virtual property, digital property, and smart property) were coined by the same author, Joshua Fairfield.[172] The notion of res digitales was then coined by Pałka.[173]

3.1.1.1 Virtual Property — the Original Notion?

Virtual property is a notion that emerged around the beginning of the millennium. Two definitions of virtual property serve as essential primers for understanding this concept — one coined by Joshua Fairfield, and one created by Hunter and Lastowka.

Fairfield defined the term as "*rivalrous, persistent, and interconnected code that mimics real world characteristics*".[174] The definition in itself does not provide many clues as to the nature of virtual property, except that is it some sort of "code" to which Fairfield attaches common law attributes. One must therefore look further into the descriptions in the article in which Fairfield explains that he means a code that is "*designed to act more like land or chattel than ideas*."[175] As examples, Fairfield lists URLs, email accounts, bank accounts, domain names or chat rooms.[176] The idea of multiple "codes" existing at the same time, with some acting as a real world property, was itself subject to scholarly criticism, namely that only one code exists, emerging as different virtual objects.[177] Furthermore, since the definition does not exactly reflect the technical reality, the examples provided by Fairfield rather appear to imply what he means by virtual property. Fairfield presumably means all digital intangibles (such as those that he listed) which may, under some circumstances, allow users the same interactions that are typical for tangible objects. Finally, Fairfield's definition was heavily based on the common law attributes of property. Accordingly, his definition may not be applicable to other jurisdictions whose requirements for something to be property may significantly differ, even in an entirely theoretical sense.

Yet, attaching the common law attributes of property to this definition is exactly what many other authors extracted from the definition. Some authors, like Blazer[178] or Nekit[179] actually followed these defining features. So we arrive at the conclusion

---

[172] See FAIRFIELD, Joshua. *Owned: Property, Privacy, and the New Digital Serfdom*. Cambridge: Cambridge University Press, 2017. ISBN 978-1107159358.

[173] See PAŁKA, Przemysław. *Virtual Property — Towards a General Theory*. 2017.

[174] FAIRFIELD, Joshua. Virtual Property. *Boston University Law Review*. 2005, vol. 85, no. 4, p. 1053.

[175] Ibid., p. 1049.

[176] Ibid., p. 1055–58.

[177] PAŁKA, Przemysław. *Virtual Property — Towards a General Theory*. 2017, p. 95.

[178] BLAZER, Charles. Blockchains and Digital Assets. *Pierce Law Review*. 2006, vol. 5, no. 1, p. 141.

[179] NEKIT, Kateryna. Social Media Account as an Object of Virtual Property. *Masaryk University Journal of Law and Technology*. 2020, vol. 14, no. 2.

that for at least some authors, virtual property is in fact tied to the attributes of rivalousness, persistency and interconnectivity.

Lastowka and Hunter came up with a more or less similar definition. According to their article, virtual property is "*entries in a database resident on a server that permits a participant's computer monitor to display images already present within the software*."[180]

Fairfield and Lastowka and Hunter were not the only ones who considered virtual property to be "code". Similarly, Charles Blazer defined virtual property as a "*persistent computer code stored on a remote resource system, where one or more persons are granted certain powers to control the computer code, to the exclusion of all other people*".[181] Looking into what he saw behind such Code, Blazer notes that virtual property may take the form of "*an email address, a website, a bidding agent, a video game character, or any number of other intangible, digital commodities*."[182]

Wian Erlank, who has authored multiple articles about virtual property, stated in a 2009 lecture that "*virtual property is what the person who hears the phrase wants it to be*."[183] This statement reflects the reality that the notion does not yet have a unified interpretation, nor does it give us any idea of the nature of virtual property. In the same lecture, Erlank referenced URLs and email addresses as examples of virtual property and also claimed that virtual property comes from virtual worlds.[184] Later on, in another article, Erlank stated that the property existing in virtual worlds was only a narrow part of virtual property and the wider understanding included other virtual objects.[185] Similarly to Erlank, Mu also describes virtual property as a notion whose meaning may vary based on the context of the specific research.[186] Consequently, Mu identifies virtual property in a stricter sense when the meaning is tied to videogames and in a broader sense where it includes URLs and internet accounts.[187]

The problems inherent with the notion of virtual property are not only that its definitions were based on the idea of a "code", but more importantly that they apparently never really stuck. Even Joshua Fairfield, who is more or less considered to be its author, never really used this notion. Furthermore, in his later works, he

---

180 LASTOWKA, Greg — HUNTER, Dan. The Laws of the Virtual Worlds. *California Law Review*. 2004, vol. 92, no. 1, p. 40.

181 BLAZER, Charles. Blockchains and Digital Assets. *Pierce Law Review*. 2006, vol. 5, no. 1, p. 141.

182 Ibid., p. 137.

183 ERLANK, Wian. Lecture: Introduction to Virtual Property. [online] 2009 [Accessed 2023-05-24]. Available at: https://papers.ssrn.com/sol3/papers.cfm?abstract_id=1491118, p. 1.

184 Ibid., p. 2.

185 ERLANK, Wian. Don't Touch My Virtual Property: Justifications for the Recognition of Virtual Property, *S. AFRICAN L.J.* 2016, vol. 133, no. 3, p. 664 footnote.

186 MU, Xiaochen. The challenge of the emergence of virtual property to the traditional legal theory and the corresponding solutions. *European Journal of Law and Technology*. 2023, vol. 14, no. 1.

187 Ibid.

continued to devise additional notions such as bitproperty[188], digital property[189] or smart property.[190] And even by the time the debate on property rights in virtual worlds had peaked, many other notions were being simultaneously used in legal literature, such as "virtual goods"[191] or "virtual items".[192]

To conclude, virtual property is a notion that can be mostly found in scholarly papers in the early 2000s focusing on the legal implications of virtual worlds. Although some definitions of virtual property are available, the understanding of the notion is much clearer via the examples given by the authors. Therefore, in a broad sense, virtual property is a notion that covers anything digital and intangible that has a certain value for users and with which the user may dispose.

3.1.1.2 Res Digitales as a New Legal Category

One more notion can only be found in legal literature, namely the term *res digitales*. This term originates from Pałka's dissertation and potentially represents a new category under private law alongside tangible and intangible things.[193] In short, res digitales is a digital variation of *res corporales* and *incorporales*. So, instead of being either tangible or intangible things, and unlike virtual property or digital assets, the notion is more of a category existing in the civil law system under which the respective digital objects, such as virtual items or cryptoassets, can be categorized.

The idea of *res digitales* did not remain in just Palka's thesis. In Legal and Regulatory Considerations for Digital Assets, authors Allen and Col. implement the idea of res digitales into their analysis of which things are capable of being subject to ownership.[194] The conclusion is that it is unclear whether res digitales objects can be owned and therefore that their physical possession is impossible.[195] Unfortunately, that is all the analysis contains on this topic.

Although comparatively little has been written about the idea of *res digitales*, it can be concluded that res digitales is a scholarly concept of creating a triad of things

---

188 FAIRFIELD, Joshua. *Southern California Law Review: Bitproperty*. 2014, vol. 88, no. 4, p. 810.

189 FAIRFIELD, Joshua. *Owned: Property, Privacy, and the New Digital Serfdom*. Cambridge: Cambridge University Press, 2017. ISBN 978-1107159358, s. 16–17; FAIRFIELD, Joshua. Tokenized: The Law of Non-Fungible Tokens and Unique Digital Property. *Indiana Law Journal*. 2022, vol. 91, no. 4.

190 FAIRFIELD, Joshua. *Owned: Property, Privacy, and the New Digital Serfdom*. Cambridge: Cambridge University Press, 2017. ISBN 978-1107159358, p. 16.

191 Used by Kenneth W. Eng in ENG, Kenneth W. Content Creators, Virtual Goods: Who Owns Virtual Property? *Cardozo arts & entertainment law journal*. 2016, vol. 34, no. 1.

192 Used by Wian Erlank in ERLANK, Wian. Don't Touch My Virtual Property: Justifications for the Recognition of Virtual Property, *S. AFRICAN L.J.* 2016, vol. 133, no. 3, p. 664 footnote.

193 PAŁKA, Przemysław. *Virtual Property — Towards a General Theory*. 2017, p. 154.

194 ALLEN, Jason G.; Rauchs, Michel; BLANDIN, Apolline; BEAR, Keith. Legal and Regulatory Considerations for Digital Assets. [online] [Accessed 2023-05-23]. Available at: https://www.jbs.cam.ac.uk/wp-content/uploads/2020/10/2020-ccaf-legal-regulatory-considerations-report.pdf, p. 25.

195 Ibid.

under civil law. And within this triad, res digitales would comprise purely digital objects which could not be physically possessed, but only controlled.

3.1.2 Notions Originating Outside the Law

It is not only legal literature that has created notions. In the end, an attempt can be observed to apply legal principles to a phenomenon existing outside of the law. Accordingly, we can see many non-legal notions finding their way into legal terminology. In this sense, the most prominent notions are (i) data, (ii) cryptoassets, and (iii) digital assets. Since the notion of digital assets will be analysed further in this chapter, I will now focus on the confusing notion of data and on the new buzzword of "cryptoassets".

3.1.2.1 Data — Lawyers' Search for the Meaning

If one notion is found that creates an enormous amount of confusion, it is the notion of data. This is quite surprising given how important data has become over the past decades for the economy. Therefore, one would expect a basic, unified understanding of the nature of data. However, this could not be further from the truth.

Data can be defined in many ways depending on the respective field of usage. This leads to confusing results where no one really knows what data is. For the purposes of the law, van Erp and Swinnen discuss whether a definition of data should be either technical, legal, or a mix of both.[196] This question is, however, left unanswered in their article, as they only outline that data must be not only legally defined, but also specified.[197] The problem is, as noted, that data may carry more meanings depending on the given field. Thus, a dozen additional possible definitions of data can be found that go beyond just a technical and legal perspective. On the one hand, it makes sense to only distinguish between the technical meaning of data, since data are used in data-driven industries. It also makes sense that a technical understanding may be at odds with the legal one given that the subject of this book is law. On the other hand, if we are to search for the true meaning of data, a more thorough analysis is required. I will first discuss the colloquial understanding of data; then I will evaluate its technical definition. Finally, I will focus on the legal literature that seeks to define this notion.

Merriam-Webster dictionary offers three definitions of data. Firstly, data is defined as "*factual information (such as measurements or statistics) used as a basis for reasoning, discussion, or calculation.*"[198] Secondly, it is "*information in digital*

[196] ERP, Sjef van and SWINNEN, Koen, 2022, The Legal Status of Co-generated Data. *Technology and Regulation.* 13 June 2022. Vol. 2022, p. 63.

[197] Ibid.

[198] Merriam Webster. Data. [online] [Accessed 2023-05-10]. Available at: https://www.merriam-webster.com/dictionary/data.

form that can be transmitted or processed." Thirdly, data is defined as "*information output by a sensing device or organ that includes both useful and irrelevant or redundant information and must be processed to be meaningful.*"

Cambridge Dictionary offers another useful definition for data, namely "*information, especially facts or numbers, collected to be examined and considered and used to help decision-making, or information in an electronic form that can be stored and used by a computer.*"[199]

These colloquial dictionary definitions provide a basic layman's understanding of the term. The definitions also help us to navigate the concept by providing examples such as statistics, or that data possess a digital/electronic form. Both dictionaries indeed offer what one usually imagines under the term "data" — statistics or numbers in digital form. However, they do not provide any leads on the concept of data, as interpreted by lawyers, computer scientists, mathematicians, sociologists or philosophers. The definitions also mix up data and information, which is something that has been subject to repeated criticism within legal literature.[200] Since this monograph is not about the relationship between the notions of data and information, or how these two notions are often used as synonyms for each other, I will not elaborate on the differences and similarities between them here.[201] The general take is that data and information are not (or at least should not be) synonymous, as information is data which carries a specific meaning.[202]

Another way to look at data is through the lens of industrial standards. According to the ISO Information Technology Vocabulary, data is a "*reinterpretable representation of information in a formalized manner suitable for communication, interpretation, or processing.*"[203] Information is then defined as "*knowledge concerning objects, such as facts, events, things, processes, or ideas, including concepts, that within a certain context has a particular meaning.*"[204] These definitions are then used in other ISO norms, for example the norm on Data Quality.[205]

As Van Erp and Swinnen point out, the ISO definition raises several more terminological questions, such as the nature of information or facts.[206] This is in fact

---

199 Cambridge Dictionary. Data. [online] [Accessed 2023-05-10]. Available at: https://dictionary.cambridge.org/dictionary/english/data.

200 POLČÁK, Radim. Informace a data v právu. *Revue pro právo a technologie*. 2016, vol. 7, no. 13.; MÍŠEK, Jakub. *Moderní regulatorní metody ochrany osobních údajů*. Brno: MUNI PRESS, 2020. ISBN 978-80-210-9737-7, p. 37–39; ERP, Sjef van and SWINNEN, Koen. The legal status of co-generated data. *Technology and Regulation*. 13 June 2022. Vol. 2022, p. 63.

201 For a deeper analysis of these two notions see BYGRAVE, Lee. Information Concepts in Law: Generic Dreams and Definitional Daylight. *Oxford Journal of Legal Studies*. 2015, vol. 35, no. 1, p. 113.

202 MÍŠEK, Jakub. *Moderní regulatorní metody ochrany osobních údajů*. Brno: MUNI PRESS, 2020. ISBN 978-80-210-9737-7, p. 38.

203 ISO/IEC 2382:2015.

204 Ibid.

205 ISO 8000-1:2022.

206 ERP, Sjef van and SWINNEN, Koen, 2022, The Legal Status of Co-generated Data. *Technology and Regulation*. 13 June 2022. Vol. 2022, p. 63.

a typical definition conundrum when it comes to data or information. By looking at the definition of data, we may extract that the idea behind the definition is that data are somehow formalized and that a purpose exists behind its collection (the aforementioned communication or processing).

The ISO norm also distinguishes between information processing (the "*systematic performance of operations upon information, that includes data processing and may include operations such as data communication and office automation*"[207]) and data processing (the "*systematic performance of operations upon data*"[208]). However, it is quite difficult to identify any major difference between these two. In the end, a broad understanding of either data or information leads to the impression that anything of relevance could be both one or the other.

The term "data" has recently been given specific meaning via EU legislation. The Data Act[209] contains a definition under which data means "*any digital representation of acts, facts or information and any compilation of such acts, facts or information, including in the form of sound, visual or audio-visual recording.*"[210] This means a specific current legal definition of this term that formally applies for at least some new data-related regulations.

Finally, many attempts are found to define data in legal scholar articles and via a several legal documents drafted by various regulatory bodies. Ritter and Mayer, for example, define data for the purpose of their paper as being "*any information recorded by electronic or digital means and* [which] *is retrievable, whether perceivable to a human or machine.*"[211] The first difference from other definitions is that the understanding of data here includes both digital and physical records. Otherwise, the abstract definition building on the notion of information does not represent much of a departure.

As for soft-law instruments, ALI-ELI has drafted the Principles for a Data Economy.[212] Under this soft-law instrument, data is defined as "*information recorded in any machine-readable format suitable for automated processing, stored in any medium, or as it is being transmitted.*"[213] We can observe multiple similarities for this legal definition with either the colloquial or industrial understanding. First, data is again understood as something existing only in a digital form. Second, the purpose of data is their processing.

---

207 ISO/IEC 2382:2015.

208 Ibid.

209 Regulation (EU) 2023/2854 of the European Parliament and of the Council of 13 December 2023 on harmonised rules on fair access to and use of data and amending Regulation (EU) 2017/2394 and Directive (EU) 2020/1828 (Data Act).

210 Article 2 (1) Data Act.

211 RITTER, Jeffrey and MAYER, Anna. Regulating Data as Property: A New Construct for Moving Forward. *Duke Law & Technology Review.* 2018, vol. 16, no. 1, p. 224.

212 ALI-ELI. Principles for a Data Economy. [online] 2021. [Accessed 2023-05-22]. Available at: https://www.europeanlawinstitute.eu/fileadmin/user_upload/p_eli/Publications/ALI-ELI_Principles_for_a_Data_Economy_Final_Council_Draft.pdf.

213 Ibid., p. 27.

The ALI-ELI Principles for a Data Economy also lay down how the defined nature of data and its scope differs from other goods or intangibles. The reason for this difference is that data is non-rivalrous (i.e., it can be multiplied)[214] and it is not sold with permission to be utilized (as opposed to IP)[215]. Moreover, the Principles explicitly state that they are not aimed at "representative data" (which represents certain value) such as cryptoassets or on "functional data" (such as computer programs), but rather on "*records of large quantities of information as an asset, resource or tradeable commodity.*"[216]

Consequently, these principles may provide basic guidance when it comes to distinguishing data from digital assets/virtual property. The difference is mostly context dependent, however, as the underlying message that that not everything that may be colloquially seen as data is in the interest of the field of law, especially when it comes to a data economy and data sharing.

Similar observations when it comes to data and digital assets may be found in the UNCITRAL's Exploratory Work on the Legal Issues Related to the Digital Economy — Reports of Events, which also distinguishes between data and digital assets based on their functions while acknowledging that digital assets consist of data.[217]

The UK Law Commission also appears to distinguish between the nature of data and digital assets. Their observation is that although everything is basically a string of data, some digital assets are more than just digital information. This conclusion serves to distinguish between what may be an object of property rights and what cannot be, and also to avoid any unwanted reforms that would make anything digital which does not reach a certain level of specificity an object of property rights.[218] Again, we can observe a difference between how the law understands data and how it understands more specific forms of data, hence digital assets.

Another indication of a difference between data and digital assets can be found in ELI's Principles on the Use of Digital Assets as Security. Specifically, ELI states that "*unlike some forms of data, digital assets can have the attribute of certainty, to the extent that they are first amenable to exclusive and substantial control and second assignable.*"[219] ELI also emphasizes that this specific document focuses on digital assets and not on the underlying data itself.[220]

---

214 Ibid., p. 8.

215 Ibid., p. 6.

216 Ibid., p. 22.

217 Exploratory Work on Legal Issues Related to the Digital Economy — Reports of Events. [online] 15. 5. 2020 [Accessed 2023-05-26]. Available at: https://uncitral.un.org/sites/uncitral.un.org/files/media-documents/uncitral/en/v2002569_1.pdf, paragraph 46.

218 UK LAW COMMISSION. Digital Assets Consultation Paper. [online] 28. 7. 2022 [Accessed 2023-07-20]. Available at: https://cloud-platform-e218f50a4812967ba1215eaecede923f.s3.amazonaws.com/uploads/sites/30/2022/07/Digital-Assets-Consultation-Paper-Law-Commission-1.pdf, p. 49.

219 European Law Institute. ELI Principles on the Use of Digital Assets as Security. [online] 28. 7. 2022 [Accessed 2023-07-20]. Available at: https://www.europeanlawinstitute.eu/fileadmin/user_upload/p_eli/Publications/ELI_Principles_on_the_Use_of_Digital_Assets_as_Security.pdf, p. 19.

220 Ibid., p. 20.

Two conclusions can be derived from this. First, digital assets are a type of data. Second, they are a specific type of data which may be subject to control and can be assigned. Therefore, at least on a legal level, data and digital assets should be treated differently, despite potentially belonging to the same semantic category.

Based on the above, we can reach the conclusion that the concept of data may carry different meanings under different scientific disciplines. Data can be a very broad and abstract notion. This means that an understanding of this term must be based on the meaning of the notion within the digital economy. This gives both legal authors and regulatory bodies wide discretion when it comes to defining the phenomenon. However, an awareness of two notable exceptions is needed here. First, data carries a specific meaning under the International Organization for Standardization (ISO). Second, a specific understanding of data under the Data Act and Data Governance Act was recently developed. This means that there is a technical understanding of data under the ISO and one clear definition of data under the EU law.

To sum up, multiple understandings exist as to the nature of data. This means that the notion itself is not static and greatly depends on the context or on specific applicable regulations. First, data may have a colloquial meaning which can be summarized as digital representations of facts, numbers or another values.

Second, data may have an industrial meaning. In that case, data is basically whatever the ISO deems it to be, and this is the meaning that will then be crucial in practice.

Third, broad literature is found on the notion of data. Here, definitions of data vary across various fields. In the past years, legal literature on data often understood it in an industrial sense.

Finally, data can also be a legal term. An official definition of data under EU law recently emerged. As a consequence, data carry the meaning assigned to it by EU policymakers in the Data Act and Data Governance Act. All these legal definitions are again framed in a strong digital economy context where the aim is to foster data sharing and to underscore how data itself does not represent a specific value as opposed to, for example, cryptoassets. And this context is what separates data from digital assets/virtual property.

Finally, it should be emphasized that data does not equal digital assets. At least not in the technical and industrial sense in which data is understood in legal literature. This will become more evident from the forthcoming analysis of the notion of digital assets. However, to give the reader an idea why these two notions are not the same, some preliminary observations must be made. Although digital assets are based on data, their understanding in legal literature is not the same. Data is what digital assets consist of and represents a far more abstract notion.

3.1.2.2 Cryptoassets

Another example of a presently trending notion finding its way into regulatory and legal texts is cryptoassets. Generally, cryptoassets are considered to be a narrower term than digital assets.[221] For instance, the Swiss Federal Department of Finance understands cryptoassets to be "*digital assets that are usually recorded on a blockchain.*"[222]

We can come across many attempts to define cryptoassets. For example, a UK policy paper defines them as "*A cryptographically secured digital representation of value or contractual rights that uses a form of distributed ledger technology and can be transferred, stored, or traded electronically.*"[223]

MiCA[224] introduced the term cryptoassets into EU law. According to the regulation, cryptoassets are "*a digital representation of* [a] *value or rights which may be transferred and stored electronically, using distributed ledger technology or similar technology.*"[225]

At first glance, both above-specified definitions have as core attributes that they are representations of value and that disposition is carried out through distributed ledger technology. The scope of the disposition then varies since the MiCA definition omits trading (although it can be argued that transfer is just a broader category under which trading may belong).

Looking at the definitions, we may also observe that they are not that different from what some consider to be digital assets. As will be explored in the following chapters, transferability and value are sometimes seen as core features of digital assets. On the one hand, this makes sense since cryptoassets are just a subcategory of digital assets. On the other hand, it begs the question of whether some definitions of digital assets are not just modelled according to the definition of digital assets. In the end, transferability is a feature inherent to cryptoassets, but not to all digital assets. Finding and shaping the legal definition of cryptoassets brings the challenge of putting the legal definitions of cryptoassets against the industry understanding of the term.

To conclude, it appears that we currently have two understandings of cryptoassets. One is the legal understanding of the notion within MiCA or under different regulations in other jurisdictions. And the other is a colloquial understanding that may or may not be completely in line with what regulation requires. But similar

221 ALLEN, Jason G.; Rauchs, Michel; BLANDIN, Apolline; BEAR, Keith. Legal and Regulatory Considerations for Digital Assets. [online] [Accessed 2023-05-23]. Available at: https://www.jbs.cam.ac.uk/wp-content/uploads/2020/10/2020-ccaf-legal-regulatory-considerations-report.pdf, p. 13.

222 Federal Department of Finance. Factsheet on Blockchain and cryptoassets in the financial sector: Switzerland's pioneering role on the international stage. [online] 24. 1. 2022 [Accessed 2023-11-29]. Available at: https://www.sif.admin.ch/sif/en/home/finanzmarktpolitik/digitalisation-financial-sector/blockchain.html.

223 UK Government. Factsheet: cryptoassets — key terms and definitions. [online] 11. 4. 2023 [Accessed 2023-05-31]. Available at: https://www.gov.uk/government/publications/economic-crime-and-corporate-transparency-bill-2022-factsheets/factsheet-cryptoassets-key-terms-and-definitions.

224 Regulation (EU) 2023/1114 of the European Parliament and of the Council of 31 May 2023 on markets in crypto-assets, and amending Regulations (EU) No 1093/2010 and (EU) no. 1095/2010 and Directives 2013/36/EU and (EU) 2019/1937 (Text with EEA relevance).

225 Article 3 Section 1., Paragraph (2) MiCA.

to data, the understanding of cryptoassets depends either on the context or the specific regulation in question.

3.1.3 Codified Notions

The final category of notions is those that exist directly within the law and even hold a legal definition. One of these notions is digital content within EU law. Digital content was first introduced in the Consumer Rights Directive[226] and defined as "*data which are produced and supplied in digital form*."[227] This definition was also used in the Digital Content Directive and the Sales of Goods Directive.

Recital 19 of the Consumer Rights Directive further explains what should be understood as digital content. According to the recital, examples of digital content are "*computer programs, applications, games, music, videos or texts*."

The notion of digital content is defined as a broad category encompassing a wide range of data made available to consumers. This encompasses any digital content that a consumer may purchase or license. The subject of digital content thus may overlap with notions such as virtual property or digital assets. However, digital content is a notion closely connected to consumer law and therefore its use is often limited in this respect. Moreover, digital content sometimes applies to intangibles other than the determined natures of virtual property and digital assets. For example, a typical example of digital content is computer programs. However, computer programs themselves are not typically considered to be virtual property or digital content. Similarly, it is unclear how digital content is related to standard examples of digital assets such as social media accounts or cryptoassets. The broad definition implies that it should be covered as well; both are, in the end, data produced and supplied in a digital form. Yet, from the recitals, it is clear that it was not intentional to cover these two digital assets.

The notion of digital content also poses a challenge as to its place within legal systems. As noted in Chapter 1, it was left to EU Member States to decide how they implement this notion. The regulation of digital content thus, on the one hand, creates a consumer legal framework when it comes to digital intangibles. The framework applies to an incredibly broad category of basically anything digital once it is offered to the consumer. On the other hand, it leaves out the important question of how these digital intangibles actually fit into the law. This means that we are left with conceptually unfinished regulation.

---

[226] Directive 2011/83/EU of the European Parliament and of the Council of 25 October 2011 on consumer rights, amending Council Directive 93/13/EEC and Directive 1999/44/EC of the European Parliament and of the Council and repealing Council Directive 85/577/EEC and Directive 97/7/EC of the European Parliament and of the Council Text with EEA relevance.

[227] Article 2, paragraph 11, Consumer Rights Directive.

The second term that has a legal definition in some jurisdictions is digital assets. This is mainly the aforementioned RUFADAA example. Additionally, other countries have introduced regulations that defined digital assets. For example, Kazakhstan recently passed a law which defined digital assets as "*property created in electronic digital form with an assigned digital code, including by using cryptography and computing,* [that is] *registered and secured by the immutability of information on the basis of distributed data platform technology.*"[228] Similarly, El Salvador is another country that has introduced the term into its legal system.[229] As a result, digital assets may have a specific meaning within a specific law in some countries.

Relatively recently, digital assets have also become a codified notion within the EU, as a result of being defined under the Data Act. According to Article 2, paragraph 32 of the Data Act, digital assets are "*elements in digital form, including applications, for which the customer has the right of use, independently from the contractual relationship with the data processing service it intends to switch from.*" Recital 83, of the Data Act further explains that digital assets are "*applications and metadata related to the configuration of settings, security, and access and control rights management, and other elements such as manifestations of virtualisation technologies, including virtual machines and containers.*" Given the cloud computing context of the definition, it appears that digital assets within the meaning of the Data Act are anything that the customer uploads to the cloud to which he or she has the right of use. In this context, the explanation in the recital is slightly misleading from the wording in Article 2, as the recital sees digital assets as "*metadata related to the configuration of settings*". Moreover, although the definition appears broad enough to accommodate some of what are colloquially understood to be digital assets (such as digital files), it appears that legislators intended to cover a specific segment of technology. In the end, it is not entirely clear what digital assets under the Data Act are supposed to be, and whether a connection exists between the colloquial understanding of digital assets and Article 2, paragraph 32 of the Data Act.

Notwithstanding the above, it is crucial to note that this is yet another instance where a distinction exists between data and digital assets.[230] However, the outcome is that we have another context in which terminology departs from the colloquial understanding.

Finally, the notion of data (as analysed below) and cryptoassets (as analysed above) recently also became codified notions under EU law. This means that both

[228] Kazakhstan: New Law Establishes Legal Framework for Digital Assets and Cryptomining. Library of Congress. [online] [Accessed 2023-07-23]. Available at: https://www.loc.gov/item/global-legal-monitor/2023-04-30/kazakhstan-new-law-establishes-legal-framework-for-digital-assets-and-cryptomining/.

[229] LEIVA, Daniel. Law of Issuance of Digital Assets in El Salvador. Consortium Legal. [online] [Accessed 2023-07-23]. Available at: https://consortiumlegal.com/en/2023/01/12/law-of-issuance-of-digital-assets-in-el-salvador/.

[230] See Recitals 84 and 86 which distinguish between data and digital assets.

notions currently have legal definitions which have to be distinguished from any colloquial understandings.

To sum up, European law now defines the notion of digital content. This notion is constructed to cover a wide variety of data offered to consumers, so it contains whatever digital a consumer might be purchasing or whatever is licensed to them. The subject of digital content overlaps with digital intangibles covered by notions such as virtual property or digital assets. However, digital content carries a specific meaning within the body of consumer protection law, which has not been used in the context of the virtual property/digital assets debate. Moreover, given its consumer background, as opposed to the financial investment context of digital assets, it appears unlikely that the term will be used in the future to merge the debate on digital intangibles.

3.2 The Notion of Digital Assets

The notion of digital assets has been in use for some time, and its use can be traced back to the 1990s.[231] The term has appeared in many fields such as computer science, economics, and law. In recent years, mostly thanks to the emergence of cryptoassets and blockchain, the term also found its way into conventional media.

The notion has covered the vast majority of intangible "things" existing in digital spaces, such as digital media (e.g., images or videos), computer files, in-game objects, all sorts of accounts and cryptoassets.[232]

At first glance, the term "digital assets" would indicate that it means any asset in a digital form. The understanding of the notion is, however, slightly more complicated. Firstly, the term "asset" may carry different meanings depending on whether it is used specifically as a legal term, economic term, or whether it is used colloquially. Secondly, the notion of digital assets lacks a unified definition and one can come across different understandings. In this subchapter, I will seek to analyse the different definitions and understandings of digital assets and find some common ground on their exact nature.

Let us begin with some remarks on the notion of "assets," since it is the core word in our studied term. As noted above, an asset can carry a different meaning in and outside of the law. Looking at assets outside of the world of law, one comes across definitions such as a "*resource with economic value that an individual, corporation, or country owns or controls with the expectation that it will provide*

[231] For example, a publication by Diane Zorich from 1999 about facilitating intellectual property rights in digital assets. See ZORICH, Diane. *Introduction to Managing Digital Assets: Options for Cultural and Educational Organizations*. Oxford: Oxford University Press, 1999. ISBN 978-0892365463.

[232] ALLEN, Jason G.; Rauchs, Michel; BLANDIN, Apolline; BEAR, Keith. Legal and Regulatory Considerations for Digital Assets. [online] [Accessed 2023-05-23]. Available at: https://www.jbs.cam.ac.uk/wp-content/uploads/2020/10/2020-ccaf-legal-regulatory-considerations-report.pdf, p. 13.

a future benefit"[233] or "*any resource or good used to generate cash flow, reduce expenses, or provide future economic benefits for an individual, government, or business.*"[234] This gives us an idea that an asset is some sort of a resource that may generate a benefit.

On the other hand, the legal understanding of the nature of assets is slightly different and, accordingly, jurisdictions can have varying interpretations and definitions. For example, under the Czech Civil Code, assets mean a person's property and debts.[235] So if the legal interpretation is simply combined with the word "digital", it would basically represent any property and liabilities in a digital form.

However, the notion of digital assets does not derive from the law. This means that when talking about digital assets, we should abandon defining the nature of assets according to the law, and instead focus on the area from which the idea of digital assets derives (i.e. the economy and investments). Accordingly, if combined with the word "digital," it is possible to imagine a resource with economic value that is digital in nature. This combination appears to be in line with what one can find under definitions of digital assets from the relevant Internet sources. For example, one source considers digital assets to be "*anything that is stored digitally and is uniquely identifiable that organizations can use to realize value. Examples of digital assets include documents, audio, videos, logos, slide presentations, spreadsheets and websites.*"[236] A combination of digital form and the colloquial/economic meaning of an asset is also the idea behind the NIST Glossary definition, according to which a digital asset is, "*Any asset that is purely digital, or is a digital representation of a physical asset.*"[237] The same attributes can also be found in a definition provided by Investopedia, according to which a digital asset is "*anything that is created and stored digitally, is identifiable and discoverable, and has or provides value.*"[238]

Based on the above, it can be concluded that digital assets on the most elementary level are:

1. something that exists in a digital form, which
2. has a value or may provide a benefit.

This is just a preliminary conclusion that gives us an understanding of what one may consider to be digital assets on the most basic level of an average Internet user.

233 BARONE, Adam. What Is an Asset? Definition, Types, and Examples. *Investopedia.* [online] 29. 3. 2023 [Accessed 2023-05-17] Available from: https://www.investopedia.com/terms/a/asset.asp.

234 What is an Asset?. *MasterClass.* [online] 7. 6. 2021 [Accessed 2023-05-17]. Available at: https://www.masterclass.com/articles/what-is-an-asset.

235 Section 495, Civil Code.

236 Digital Assets. *Gartner Glossary.* [online] [Accessed 2023-05-17]. Available at: https://www.gartner.com/en/finance/glossary/digital-assets.

237 Computer Security Resource Centre. Digital Asset. [online] [Accessed 2023-05-17]. Available at: https://csrc.nist.gov/glossary/term/digital_asset.

238 FRANKENFIELD, Jake. What is a Digital Asset?. *Investopedia.* [online] 30. 6. 2022 [Accessed 2023-05-17]. Available at: https://www.investopedia.com/terms/d/digital-asset-framework.asp.

That is why in this analysis I will also look into legal scholar writings on the nature of digital assets.

Multiple legal papers have been written about digital assets. The authors usually sought to define digital assets. Therefore, numerous papers are found in which the authors give a definition of digital assets, for example, as "*anything that can be stored and transmitted electronically (using a computer) that can be owned and thus, can have ownership and usage rights associated with it.*"[239] Or we see papers that just give examples of what the author considers to be digital assets. Lehavi, for example, simply states that digital assets are a "*broad plethora of resources, such as email and social media accounts, electronic media in digital form such as music, videos, and books, or reward points earned by persons participating in a retail program or using a certain credit card,*"[240] without searching for the deeper meaning behind the term. The Table below indicates the multiple definitions collated here from legal literature.

Digital assets according to legal scholars:

Author	Definition
Luis-Daniel Ibáñez	"(...) anything that can be stored and transmitted electronically (using a computer) that **can be owned** and thus, can have ownership and usage rights associated with it. Due to the diversity and variability of digital assets, ranging from **audio files to email accounts**, the scope of our report only relates to digital assets that can be tokenized using a cryptographic protocol, or so-called **crypto assets**."[241]
Natalie Banta	"Digital assets include an individual's **email accounts, personal webpages, blogs, social networking sites, documents, videos, or photo storage sites**."[242]

[239] IBÁÑEZ, Luis-Daniel. Blockchains and Digital Assets. EU Blockchain Forum. [online] 2018 [Accessed 2023-05-24]. Available at: https://www.eublockchainforum.eu/sites/default/files/research-paper/blockchains_and_digital_assets_june_version.pdf.

[240] LEHAVI, Amnon. Intellectual Property, Data, and Digital Assets. In: LEHAVI, Amnon. *Property Law in a Globalizing World*. Cambridge University Press, 2019. ISBN 9781108595391, p. 200.

[241] IBÁÑEZ, Luis-Daniel. Blockchains and Digital Assets. EU Blockchain Forum. [online] 2018 [Accessed 2023-05-24]. Available at: https://www.eublockchainforum.eu/sites/default/files/research-paper/blockchains_and_digital_assets_june_version.pdf.

[242] BANTA, Natalie. Inherit the Cloud: The Role of Private Contracts in Distributing or Deleting Digital Assets at Death. *Fordham Law Review*, vol. 83, no. 2, p. 801.

Amnon Lehavi	"The term digital assets may refer to a broad plethora of resources, such as **email and social media accounts, electronic media in digital form such as music, videos, and books, or reward points** earned by persons participating in a retail program or using a certain credit card."[243]
John Connor	"... any digital file on a person's computer, as well as online accounts and memberships"[244]
Jamie B. Hopkins	"... information stored in an intangible medium on computers or on another computer-related technology" [245]
Laura McCarthy	"... information stored in an intangible medium on computers or other computer-related technology"[246]
Paweł SZWAJDLER	"... digital data or, electronic records belonging to their possessors (...) examples of digital assets are files such as movies, images, texts, sounds, games, etc."[247]

This table above illustrates how legal scholars understand digital assets. Multiple conclusions are possible from such a collection of views. First, some authors have sought to devise a proper definition, while others completely omit this step and only list examples of what they consider to be digital assets. The latter is not necessarily unwelcome, since it likely offers the reader a more specific idea of what digital assets are in comparison with a mere vague definition.

Second, the definitions are often based on "information" or a "file" in electronic form. This appears to represent each author's attempt to describe the current technical reality. The problem here is that such a definition can often appear both forcefully technical and vague. The definitions also do not work with attributes such as value or transferability which, as will be demonstrated below, is the approach adopted by some regulatory bodies and legal groups.

243 LEHAVI, Amnon. Intellectual Property, Data, and Digital Assets. In: LEHAVI, Amnon. *Property Law in a Globalizing World.* Cambridge University Press, 2019. ISBN 9781108595391, p. 200.

244 CONNOR, John. Digital Life after Death: The Issue of Planning for a Person's Digital Assets after Death. *Estate Planning & Community Property Law Journal.* 2011, (2).

245 HOPKINS, Jamie. Afterlife in the Cloud: Managing a Digital Estate. *Hastings Science and Technology Law Journal.* 2013, vol. 5, no. 2.

246 MCCARTHY, Laura. Digital Assets and Intestacy. *Boston University Journal of Science and Technology Law*. 2015, vol. 21, no. 2.

247 SZWAJDLER, Paweł. "Digital assets and inheritance law: How to create the fundamental principles of [a] digital succession system?" Online. *International Journal of Law and Information Technology.* 2023, vol. 31, no. 2, p. 146.

One definition that stands out is by Ibanez[248], since the crucial feature is that digital assets are capable of being the subject of ownership. Here I can see two issues. First, one must make an assessment of whether certain digital intangibles can be owned. Second, as is apparent from the previous chapter, the outcome of such an assessment will quite often be inconclusive.

As noted, some authors merely give examples of digital assets as opposed to defining the term. In legal literature, we can even find a more radical approach, namely not offering any definition or examples at all. This, for example, is the case with Fairfield's article on NFTs, where it is left to the reader to deduce the meaning of digital assets. Indeed, he only occasionally mentions examples of digital assets, such as avatars in online games, or islands in the video game Animal Crossing, or a Facebook page.[249]

Contrary to the broad definitions offered by legal scholars as demonstrated by the table above, the Cambridge Centre for Alternative Finance came up with much more narrow understanding of the term.[250] One the outcomes of their legal analysis was the creation of two categories in this respect — digital assets and "new" digital assets.[251] The notion of new digital assets reflects new objects in distributed ledger systems and is characterized as being 1) expressive, 2) controllable via cryptographic keys and 3) compatible.[252] The authors of the analysis argue that this new category should not be treated as a "*stand-alone category for the purposes of legal categorization.*" However, if that is the case, it appears somewhat confusing to even identify this new category and call it "new" digital assets in the first place. This only adds more confusion to an already chaotic debate.

Recently, a several attempts were made to offer a legal definition of digital assets in studies/consultations provided by a number of respected institutions. Specifically, four institutions were tasked with tackling the topic of digital assets, which also included the creation of a definition for the purposes of each published document. UNIDROIT's study was called "Digital Assets and Private Law". The European Law Institute issued their "Principles on the Use of Digital Assets as Security". The UK Law Commission adopted a "Consultation Paper" regarding digital assets. Finally, the European Commission addressed digital assets in their initiative on Web 4.0. I will not analyse the subject and main findings of the three documents here, since that is beyond the scope of this chapter. I will only focus on the respective

248 IBÁÑEZ, Luis-Daniel. Blockchains and Digital Assets. EU Blockchain Forum. [online] 2018 [Accessed 2023-05-24]. Available at: https://www.eublockchainforum.eu/sites/default/files/research-paper/blockchains_and_digital_assets_june_version.pdf.

249 FAIRFIELD, Joshua. Tokenized: The Law of Non-Fungible Tokens and Unique Digital Property. *Indiana Law Journal*. 2022, vol. 91, no. 4, pp. 1264–65.

250 ALLEN, Jason G.; Rauchs, Michel; BLANDIN, Apolline; BEAR, Keith. Legal and Regulatory Considerations for Digital Assets. [online] [Accessed 2022-08-27]. Available at: https://www.jbs.cam.ac.uk/wp-content/uploads/2020/10/2020-ccaf-legal-regulatory-considerations-report.pdf.

251 Ibid., p. 13.

252 Ibid.

understandings of the nature of digital assets, since they were the subject of all three documents. The three definitions are outlined in the table below:

Digital assets according to selected legal documents:

UNIDROIT "Digital Assets and Private Law"	"an **electronic record** which is capable of being **subject to control**"[253]
European Law Institute "ELI Principles on the Use of Digital Assets as Security"	"... any **record or representation of value** that fulfils the following criteria: (i) it is exclusively stored, displayed and administered **electronically**, on or through a virtual platform or database, including where it is a record or representation of a real-world, tradeable asset, and whether or not the digital asset itself is held directly or through an account with an intermediary; (ii) it is **capable of being subject to a right of control, enjoyment or use,** regardless of whether such rights are legally characterised as being of a proprietary, obligational or other nature; and (iii) it is **capable of being transferred** from one party to another, including by way of voluntary disposition"[254]
UK Law Commission "Digital Assets Consultation Paper"	"Any **asset** that is represented **digitally or electronically**. There are many different types of digital assets, not all of which will be capable of attracting personal property rights."[255]
European Commission "An EU initiative on Web 4.0 and virtual worlds: a head-start in the next technological transition"	"Digital representation of **value** that can be **traded, transferred or used** for payment. It has specific usage rights and can include anything from cryptocurrencies to digital art and other forms of intellectual property."[256]

At first glance, it is apparent that unlike the conclusions by legal scholars, the digital assets in these documents are defined on a more abstract level and do not

[253] UNIDROIT. Digital Assets and Private Law. [online] April 2023 [Accessed 2023-07-20]. Available at: https://www.unidroit.org/wp-content/uploads/2023/04/C.D.-102-6-Principles-on-Digital-Assets-and-Private-Law.pdf.

[254] European Law Institute. ELI Principles on the Use of Digital Assets as Security. [online] 28. 7. 2022 [Accessed 2023-07-20]. Available at: https://www.europeanlawinstitute.eu/fileadmin/user_upload/p_eli/Publications/ELI_Principles_on_the_Use_of_Digital_Assets_as_Security.pdf, p. 17.

[255] UK LAW COMMISSION. Digital Assets Consultation Paper. [online] 28. 7. 2022 [Accessed 2023-07-20]. Available at: https://cloud-platform-e218f50a4812967ba1215eaecede923f.s3.amazonaws.com/uploads/sites/30/2022/07/Digital-Assets-Consultation-Paper-Law-Commission-1.pdf, p. ix.

[256] EUROPEAN COMMISSION. "An EU initiative on Web 4.0 and virtual worlds: a head start in the next technological transition." {COM(2023) 442 final}. 2023, p. 85

confuse definitions with examples. This is not surprising given that the working groups were tasked with preparing an analysis — thus a definition of the subject of the analysis was required.

It is also apparent that most of the documents seek to define digital assets as something "digital" or "electronic" which has 1) value 2) is transferable and 3) is subject to control. This is important, as two of the provided definitions likely would not cover the examples presented in the first table. This is actually acknowledged by UNIDROIT, who specifically distinguish between the colloquial understanding of digital assets and their legal understanding as something that requires control.[257] The requirement for control is also not something unique to these documents. For example, the proposed amendments to the Uniform Commercial Code in the Unites States also use the concept of control when defining "controllable electronic records."[258]

What is understood as control may slightly differ. Some consensus appears to be found that control is a factual concept that may carry legal consequences.[259] But at the same time, all the respective documents that use the concept seek to grasp it in their own manner. For example, the concept of control in ELI's definition is explained as "*the right to access and enjoy the non-traditional form of value that a digital asset embodies*."[260] This should include the possibility of transferring assets which are also a defining attribute.[261] ELI gives examples of what would fall within their definition. This would, for example, include internet accounts and cryptoassets. However, the limit here is that nothing in contracts prevents the assignment of such digital assets.[262] On the other hand, the definition is meant to exclude data stored in accounts.[263] I will focus more on the understanding of control and its relevance for digital assets in the next chapter.

Looking at the definitions themselves, we can observe that they seek to be as broad as possible. For example, ELI's definition includes anything digital which

---

257 UNIDROIT. Digital Assets and Private Law. [online] April 2023 [Accessed 2023-07-20]. Available at: https://www.unidroit.org/wp-content/uploads/2023/04/C.D.-102-6-Principles-on-Digital-Assets-and-Private-Law.pdf, p. 17.

258 Article 12, paragraph (1) of the revised UCC.

259 This is what both UNIDROIT and UK Law Commission specifically explain as their understanding of control — see UNIDROIT. Digital Assets and Private Law. [online] April 2023 [Accessed 2023-07-20]. Available at: https://www.unidroit.org/wp-content/uploads/2023/04/C.D.-102-6-Principles-on-Digital-Assets-and-Private-Law.pdf, p.38 and UK LAW COMMISSION. Digital Asset: Final Report. [online] 27. 6. 2023 [Accessed 2023-08-11]. Available at: https://cloud-platform-e218f50a4812967ba1215eaecede923f.s3.amazonaws.com/uploads/sites/30/2023/06/Final-digital-assets-report-FOR-WEBSITE-2.pdf, pp. 24–25; 84.

260 European Law Institute. ELI Principles on the Use of Digital Assets as Security. [online] 28. 7. 2022 [Accessed 2023-07-20]. Available at: https://www.europeanlawinstitute.eu/fileadmin/user_upload/p_eli/Publications/ELI_Principles_on_the_Use_of_Digital_Assets_as_Security.pdf, pp.18–19.

261 Ibid.

262 Ibid., p. 19.

263 Ibid.

fulfils the respective criteria. The definition was not created by examining numerous examples and looking for common attributes. Rather, it stated some functional features for digital assets and then delineated what might fall within the given definition. However, it appears that ELI's own explanation is contradictory to their definition. Chiefly, it is unclear why data in accounts would not fall within the definition, since the possibility exists that it may fulfil the given attributes. The definition is also very restrictive and requires a precise case-by-case analysis, which might be impractical. On the other hand, the definition does not lead to any required reforms of current laws.

The UK Law Commission decided on a broad and simplifying definition. This is logical given that they needed a broader subject to analyse, since they sought to focus on the category of digital assets as a whole.[264] In order to provide a comprehensive analysis, they looked into a wide range of digital assets, including crypto-tokens, NFTs and domain names, as well as carbon emissions trading schemes and in-game objects. Thus, we see that the subject of their consultation is again anything digital. What we can take from their approach is that digital assets are a broad category that does not fall under one legal category if analysed. Specifically, even though the UK Law Commission sees digital assets as a broad category, they do not conclude that all digital assets fit their third category of things.[265] This makes the terminology again confusing, as the UK Law Commission calls the third category of thing "data objects" which are not synonymous with digital assets. However, this finding is a next step to the original problem highlighted in this chapter, namely the definition of digital assets.

The definition used by the European Commission represents another very broad understanding of the term, since it is supposed to include "*anything from cryptocurrencies to digital art and other forms of intellectual property*." Moreover, it again associates digital assets with value. What is different is that the definition requires a payment to be made. Unfortunately, it is not clear what is meant by payment. It also appears that the definition was again crafted with cryptoassets in mind. Only this time the Commission incorporated not only cryptocurrency but also NFTs. That is likely why the definition references digital art and intellectual property. I believe that this is an example of defining digital assets in a specific context, and thus can be anything that the authors need it to be for the purposes of whatever they are writing.

Looking at all four definitions, we can observe two different approaches. One defines digital assets as broadly as possible (which is what the UK Law Commission did), but acknowledging that not everything deemed digital assets may be a thing in the legal sense. The other is to narrow down the broad colloquial understanding

---

264 UK LAW COMMISSION. Digital Assets Consultation Paper. [online] 28. 7. 2022 [Accessed 2023-07-20]. Available at: https://cloud-platform-e218f50a4812967ba1215eaecede923f.s3.amazonaws.com/uploads/sites/30/2022/07/Digital-Assets-Consultation-Paper-Law-Commission-1.pdf, pp. 3–4.

265 Ibid., p. 109.

of digital assets into what can probably be seen as a legal definition with attributes that may be useful to the law (which is control and transferability). Both approaches nevertheless lead to the result that no matter how digital assets are defined, legal analysis still needs to be conducted to determine whether a specific digital asset fits into a particular legal category. The narrowed down definition appears to only work in the context of looking for certain functions or principles that may be applied within the existing framework.

Finally, it should be noted that aside from legal scholars and regulatory groups, digital assets are also associated with fiduciary access to digital assets and RUFADAA has a definition of the term. According to the Act, digital assets are: "*an electronic record in which an individual has a right or interest. The term does not include an underlying asset or liability unless the asset or liability is itself an electronic record.*" However, this is a very specific example of a law that defines what it applies to within a clear jurisdiction. More examples of legal definitions of digital assets are found in the previous chapter.

To conclude, digital assets are a broad category of digital intangibles which can cover almost anything we encounter online. Attempts have been made to define the term in legal literature; however, no consensus is presently found on a definition. We can, however, observe a trend of associating digital assets with value and control in recent legal documents created by bodies such as UNIDROIT. This being said, the term still carries a broad colloquial meaning evident mostly via authors that have similar ideas about specific examples of digital assets.

At this point, digital assets may have multiple meanings. For one, a colloquial understanding of the term. Or jurisdictions which have adopted a definition of digital assets for the purposes of their specific laws where the notion carries a specific meaning within that law. Or the current trend of introducing a legal definition of digital assets through attributes such as "value", "transfer" and "control". Consequently, any debate on digital assets requires a careful initial understanding of the respective nature of digital assets, since the notion currently suffers from considerable subjective and fragmented interpretation.

A number of questions naturally arise as to the present fragmented and subjective nature of our understanding of digital assets. For example — how does the notion of digital assets fit into the wider pool of various existing notions? Is it same notion as data? Or the same as virtual property? Are digital assets res digitales? The following paragraphs will try to shed some light on the differences between the examined notions.

3.3 Are Digital Assets and Virtual Property Same?

The two notions that can be concluded to have the most similarity are digital assets and virtual property. The UK Law Commission also references the available legal literature on virtual property in its Consultation Paper on digital assets.[266] Furthermore, these two notions have some explicitly acknowledged overlap in legal literature. For instance, Connor considers virtual property and digital assets to be synonymous.[267] Van Erp writes about both virtual property and digital assets being similar terms, both relating to information.[268] Nekit uses the notion of digital assets to define virtual property rights.[269]

Both notions have a broad and a narrow meaning that appears across literature. In their broad meaning, both digital assets and virtual property refer to a wide category of "intangibles" existing in the digital environment, be it in-game objects, accounts or cryptocurrency. However, both notions also have their own restricted meaning in which several differences can be observed:

First, the context in which the notions are used differs slightly. Virtual property is linked to virtual worlds and to the ownership existing inside these worlds, whereas digital assets are used in much broader context. Virtual property is also not linked to blockchain and cryptocurrency as much as digital assets.

Second, the definition of digital assets according to soft-law documents such as ELI Principles or the UNIDROIT study is much stricter than "every intangible asset in cyberspace". The scope of soft-law instruments is thus limited to those digital assets that are transferable and are capable of control.

Based on the above, I would argue that virtual property and digital assets represent an essentially identical category and are in effect the same term. The difference is simply the time it took for these notions to find their way into legal literature, and that digital assets, contrary to virtual property, are a notion that appears to be finding its way into actual laws. But simply looking at what many authors imagined under these two terms, I conclude that the colloquial understanding is the same.

3.4 Are Digital Assets and Data the Same?

Similarly to virtual property, digital assets and data are also related notions. However, as noted in the above analysis, these two notions need to be understood as two different concepts used in a different (regulatory or legal) context.

266 Law Commission. Digital Assets — Consultation Paper. [online] [Accessed 2023-05-08] Available at: https://cloud-platform-e218f50a4812967ba1215eaecede923f.s3.amazonaws.com/uploads/sites/30/2022/07/Digital-Assets-Consultation-Paper-Law-Commission-1.pdf, p. 2.

267 CONNOR, John. Digital Life after Death: The Issue of Planning for a Person's Digital Assets after Death. *Estate Planning & Community Property Law Journal*. 2011, (2), p. 303.

268 ERP, Sjef van. Ownership of Data: The Numerus Clausus of Legal Objects. Revised and expanded version of an article, Ownership of Digital Assets, originally written as a contribution to a Festschrift. [online]. [Accessed 2023-08-31]. Available at: https://scholarship.law.wm.edu/propertyjournal/6/, p. 243.

269 NEKIT, Kateryna. Social Media Account as an Object of Virtual Property. *Masaryk University Journal of Law and Technology*. 2020, vol. 14, no. 2, p. 208.

Apart from the difference between the notions found in the regulatory texts referenced above, we can also find cases where legal authors distinguish between the two notions. For example, Lehavi differentiates between data and digital assets.[270] To do this, he borrows the understanding of notions from Banta and van Erp. The problem is that it is not entirely clear what the actual difference is here, since digital assets are defined through examples (as borrowed from Banta) and data only as information stored at a data carrier (as borrowed from van Erp).[271] This does not provide readers any clue as to what they should imagine under the two notions. However, the important thing is that at least for Lehavi, data and digital assets are not the same thing.

Consequently, I argue that digital assets and data should not be understood as being the same under the law. Although the literature surrounding both notions deal with similar topics — most importantly with the ownership issues concerning one or the other — these notions must be understood as two different categories.

Naturally, similarities are found between the two. This is mostly in the fact that both are intangible in nature and exist in digital space. However, the category of data is much broader than digital assets.

Digital assets are valuable digital intangibles in a specific form, such as digital media, accounts and cryptoassets. Data, however, is mostly (in its industrial sense) raw facts, tables or numbers. Its nature is far more dynamic than digital assets, as it is collected, processed and stored. Conversely, digital assets (where transferable and controllable) are traded, stored and managed.

To sum up, digital assets comprise data (similarly as everything in cyberspace). But digital assets are a specific object. Colloquially, when talking about data (especially manufactured data sets), one imagines fairly different objects than when speaking about digital assets.

3.5 Concluding Remarks

Based on the aforementioned, it appears that all the notions describe a phenomenon that is *essentially* the same. The word "essentially" here is crucial. It should emphasize that the terms are *not exactly* the same, but rather that what they mean is similar in its core. If we look at the examples the authors typically give to describe what these notions cover, we can observe that the examples are almost always identical. Often the only difference is the time when these terms were coined. The early 2000s term of virtual property does not include cryptoassets simply because cryptoassets were not widely known or in use during those times.

[270] LEHAVI, Amnon. Intellectual Property, Data, and Digital Assets. In: LEHAVI, Amnon. *Property Law in a Globalizing World.* Cambridge University Press, 2019. ISBN 9781108595391.

[271] Ibid., p. 200.

On the other hand, it is important to note that the context behind all these notions differs. As a result, we can have notions whose objects are essentially same. But the context in which these notions are used is different.

3.6 The Impact of Terminological Fragmentation on the Application of Laws and Regulations

The underlying issue in this chapter is whether the parallel existence of multiple notions leads to confusion and whether a unified term would be beneficial to either solving conceptual or regulatory questions.

Looking at the background of the applicable notions, it is apparent that the context in which the notions are used may significantly differ. It also appears that the creation of such notions is closely tied to the times when they first appeared, as all serve as a response to technological changes. Virtual property emerged when virtual worlds appeared. Digital assets appeared with the rise in popularity of cryptoassets. And the debate surrounding data is a consequence of the current data-driven economy.

So what are the consequences of such terminological fragmentation? In the following paragraphs I will argue that the current state may lead to the improper application of the law — but mostly to potentially imperfect regulation.

The first consequence of this terminological confusion might be **an incorrect application of the law**. The law is largely about application of (often vague) rules to specific situations. However, we are seeking to apply an unanchored notion to legal categories that do not completely fit their meaning.[272] These, in most cases, are legal categories either from a property law, data protection or intellectual property framework.[273] The result is that when applying the law to digital assets, data, virtual property, or any other notion that carries a similar meaning, we must first understand what these notions are, and only then we can apply legal rules. But this is an incredibly difficult task when we have to rely mostly on semantic or colloquial meanings. Moreover, the problem appears to be just an extension of a fairly old issue of categorizing and differentiating between data and information in the world of law. Thus, we may reach the conclusion that fitting any of the notions under one specific legal category is simply not possible or it may be confusing. For example, it has often been stated that data or information cannot be owned. However, the definition of both data and information is often rather vague and broad as demonstrated in the previous subchapters. This means that under some of the definitions anything can be data or information, even objects that are quite specific and do not only represent

272 BIRNHACK, Michael a MORSE, Tal. Digital remains: property or privacy? Online. *International journal of law and information technology*. 2022, vol. 30, no. 3, p. 281.

273 Ibid.

raw data. In the end, such generalisation may lead to the misapplication of the law if lawyers, judges or legislators simply assume that no data can be owned even though the object in question actually could have been owned.

The aforementioned also opens up one very important question — does everything that falls into one category (like digital assets or data) fall under the same legal category (such as a thing or personal data), or do individual examples fall into different legal categories or different legal frameworks? And if they fall under different categories, what is the point of having one umbrella term? When dealing with individual cases, it may not matter whether a superior category applies, especially since such a superior category will not be a legal one. For example, most categories give broad examples such as video game objects, bitcoins or computer files. However, just by looking at all the examples it is obvious that it may be hard to fit them all under one legal category. Even the category of digital content, which is a legal category, is so broad that we can argue that one cannot say "digital content = a thing" or "digital content = copyrighted work". In the end, the notion of digital content works in a consumer-specific context, but not for another set of rules. I think that no matter how digital intangibles are termed, the notion only works as far as illustrating the legal and regulatory issues concerning the respective uncertain legal framework and legal protections — in other words, to show that the law works slightly differently online than offline.

Moreover, the fragmentation of legal literature may cause important information or research on a topic to be overlooked by those applying the law — be it attorneys or judges. Or even by academics themselves. Therefore, unifying the debate may have positive results in the sense that everybody will be on the same page.

However, far bigger consequences may lie with future regulation. Currently, we see calls for the regulation of digital assets, data, digital content, cryptoassets and technologies that are connected to the topic, such as blockchain or AR/VR. In the end, the fragmentation of notions may lead to the fragmentation of regulation. This, in the end, may mean such regulation overlaps and becomes mutually exclusive.

The remaining question is what to do with the notion of digital assets from a legal point of view. Here, I see two options:

1. We may separate those digital assets to which respective laws can be applied (which is what UNIDROIT did in their Principles and how they constructed their definition). Then we would have a category which can function under current private law and a category that does not fulfil legal requirements. For determining to which law digital assets might be easily applied we would only need a further clarification on how solve the respective practical matters. This option does not shift current laws, which may be both an advantage and disadvantage, depending on how the respective viewpoint about making sufficient changes to the existing legal system.
2. Or we may take the bulk of what digital assets represent colloquially and create a legal framework to fit their respective nature, which would constitute a new legal field. Such a legal framework could have similarities with property laws

or maybe with trust funds or intellectual property. That is for another debate. However, this change would address and thoroughly challenge their nature and we would not have speculated on defining digital assets and how the law applies to them. This again might be a viable solution for some and a bad solution for others.

To conclude, the fragmentation of terminology, coupled with the broad understanding of applicable notions, mostly opens up the question of whether such an umbrella term should be narrowed down in order to ease the application of the law. In this sense, it is logical that UNIDROIT or ELI opted for a definition that drafts certain unifying features of digital assets in order to make the application of the law more universal (whether their respective definitions match the understanding of the terms is for another debate).

Finally, one solution (for both future research and regulation) is to clearly distinguish between specified and unspecified data. Once the law and regulations make an explicit distinction between the two, many debates on what is and is not data can be put to rest and we can start discussing options for the separate categories. Yes, the distinction might never perfectly capture the technological reality. However, with the current state-of-the-art of the whole data economy and Internet, and with constant technological developments, we might never find a perfect solution. Gaps between the law and technology may always be found. However, having at least some set of rules is, in my opinion, better that the current state.

4 THE LEGAL NATURE OF DIGITAL ASSETS ACCORDING TO CZECH LAW

As numerous authors have pointed out, the applicable legal framework for various digital intangibles remains uncertain.[274] Digital intangibles are typically governed by contracts and licenses that are either standardised or customised to the specific circumstances. Service providers typically choose intellectual property law as their primary means of protection. This means that while property in the "offline" world is protected by the traditional property framework, everything online is usually governed as intellectual property. As a result, the two property frameworks — traditional and intellectual — became two separate legal fields that appear to work on an exclusive basis.[275]

Another angle can be found for how to examine the current situation. The rules of what one can do with digital assets (and with any other digital intangibles that would not fall under the digital assets category) are set by the companies who run the respective platforms and not by legislators. In practice this means that answers to the questions such as "Can I transfer my reward points?" or "Do my heirs inherit my social media account?" start with "It depends on the contract/terms and conditions."

Nonetheless, many authors tried to challenge this prevailing practice over the past two decades, either by advocating for the application of the traditional property legal framework or by suggesting new regulatory concepts, such as quasi-property for the digital intangibles. The application of a traditional property framework appeared even more pressing since some digital intangibles such as cryptoassets or raw data cannot easily be fit into the intellectual property framework, as they do not pass the requirements for copyrighted works. Therefore, in this chapter, in order to determine its limits, I will try to apply the Czech property law framework (including intellectual property) to digital assets.

As follows from the previous chapter, digital assets are a diverse group of various digital objects, which makes their categorization under the law complicated, since a thorough analysis of each digital asset must be conducted in order to decide its respective legal nature. Accordingly, the premise of this chapter is that digital

---

274 This is largely explored in Chapter 2.

275 ERP, Sjef van. Ownership of Data: The Numerus Clausus of Legal Objects. Revised and expanded version of an article, Ownership of Digital Assets, originally written as a contribution to a Festschrift. [online]. [Accessed 2023-08-31]. Available at: https://scholarship.law.wm.edu/propertyjournal/6/, p. 238.

assets are highly context and usage dependant and thus, it is not possible to categorize them all under the same category.[276] In other words, the hypothesis is: just because something can be colloquially considered to be a digital asset does not automatically mean that the whole group falls under the same legal category.

Many legal categories are found under which digital assets might potentially fall, and many legal fields can apply to digital assets depending on the context. In order to narrow down the scope of this chapter I will explore on a more general level the following legal categories for digital assets — intangible thing, copyrighted work, property and assets, and inheritance. Only after establishing if a digital asset falls under one or another of these categories will it be possible to proceed to the next phase, i.e. whether digital assets can be an object of traditional or intellectual property rights (or whether they may be bequeathed upon death and so on).

Then, in order to test the premise of this chapter, I will try to categorize three selected digital assets that are often listed as examples of this notion and analyse whether they fit under the above-selected categories of the Czech private law framework, i.e. whether each of these three digital assets can be an object of property rights. At the same, this chapter will seek to identify any gaps in the current legal framework and analyse whether Czech traditional and intellectual property laws allow for certain property rights to apply to these digital assets.

The aim of this chapter is to discuss whether Czech property law, which is significantly influenced by the Austrian civil code, can be applicable to digital assets and to what extent. In other words, to identify the limits of the Czech property law framework in relation to digital assets with an emphasis on ownership. Traditional property frameworks vary among jurisdictions. Not only does this mean that what is possible in one jurisdiction may not work in another, but it also means that, unlike with tangible things, different levels of protection can apply for digital assets in different countries. Moreover, the question is also whether the default rules of property law ownership are even possible to apply when it comes to something that is not only intangible in its nature, but usually limited by the respective technology. I will also address the concept of control, which is linked to digital assets and is sometimes considered their defining feature.

4.1 Digital Assets as (Intangible) Things

One of the issues connected to digital assets is whether they can be an object of property rights including ownership, since traditionally only things could be an object of

[276] ALLEN, Jason G.; Rauchs, Michel; BLANDIN, Apolline; BEAR, Keith. Legal and Regulatory Considerations for Digital Assets. [online] [Accessed 2023-05-23]. Available at: https://www.jbs.cam.ac.uk/wp-content/uploads/2020/10/2020-ccaf-legal-regulatory-considerations-report.pdf, p. 15.

these rights.[277] This requirement is what creates an obstacle for those jurisdictions which only recognize tangible objects as things and what has led to suggestions such as Fairfield's attempt to treat property as information and not a thing.[278] This is also why the UK Law Commission is advocating for recognizing a third category of things under which digital assets may be categorized.[279]

Czech law follows the traditional requirement for an object of property rights to be a thing. **This precondition has consequences in the area of property rights (such as that only a thing may be a pledge), and also in other areas.** For instance, a deposit presumes that the depositary takes over a thing to hold for the depositor.[280] Similarly, a security is provided through creating a pledge.[281] However, as already noted, only a thing may serve as a pledge. Therefore, in order to use a digital asset for the purposes of deposit or security, it must a thing in the first place. Finally, according to Section 15 of the Czech Commercial code, only a thing may be the object of a contribution to a business company.

Notwithstanding the above, with the introduction of the new Civil Code, this requirement has been expanded to include both tangible and intangible things. Moreover, the Czech Civil Code was created with the idea of having a wide category of things so the interpretation of this category may be flexible and broad enough to accommodate anything intangible, including, for example, copyrighted works.[282] This should, in theory, allow for the application of traditional property law to digital assets. Unfortunately, the idea of a wide category of things did not result in a broader application to include intangible objects. Conversely, numerous unresolved questions appeared when it came to the actual application. A few examples of this uncertainty include the below issues:

1. Intangible things include "*rights whose nature allows it and other things without corporeal substance.*"[283] However, this in many cases creates a duality, with an object that may be an intangible thing and a right to this object which can also be classified as an intangible thing. Applied to digital assets, imagine one has a gaming account. What is the intangible thing in that case — the account or the rights to this account? Or both?

---

277 ERP, Sjef van. Ownership of Data: The Numerus Clausus of Legal Objects. Revised and expanded version of an article, Ownership of Digital Assets, originally written as a contribution to a Festschrift. [online]. [Accessed 2023-08-31]. Available at: https://scholarship.law.wm.edu/propertyjournal/6/, p. 235–238.

278 FAIRFIELD, Joshua. Bitproperty. *Southern California Law Review*. 2014, vol. 88, no. 4, p. 810.

279 UK LAW COMMISSION. Digital Assets: Final Report. [online] 27. 6. 2023 [Accessed 2023-08-31]. Available at: https://cloud-platform-e218f50a4812967ba1215eaecede923f.s3.amazonaws.com/uploads/sites/30/2023/06/Final-digital-assets-report-FOR-WEBSITE-2.pdf, p. ix, p. 12.

280 Article 2402, Czech Civil Code.

281 Article 2012, Czech Civil Code.

282 Explanatory Memorandum. [online] [Accessed 2023-09-15]. Available at: http://obcanskyzakonik.justice.cz/images/pdf/Duvodova-zprava-NOZ-konsolidovana-verze.pdf, p. 117.

283 Section 496 paragraph 2 Civil Code.

2. Although the Civil Code recognizes intangible things, it is unclear whether classifying something as an intangible thing actually has legal consequences. This is due to Section 979 of the Civil Code, which states that although property rights apply to both tangible and intangible things, they only apply to rights to the extent permitted by their nature. Moreover, a consensus evidently exists between civil law commentators that the wording here is actually incorrect and that property rights should only apply in a limited manner not only to rights, but also to intangible things.[284] As a result, legislators created an inconsistency when on the one hand, we have a broad category of things, on the other, property rights do not apply.[285] Therefore, the practical implications of being categorised as an intangible thing remain unclear.
3. It is also unclear whether something can be categorized as a thing and a copyrighted work at the same time. Or, even if it could, it appears the same object cannot be protected by both copyright and property rights, since the Civil Code indirectly excludes this.[286] Yet, digital assets such as in-game objects, are subject to intellectual property rights. Thus, users may not obtain property rights or apply proprietary protections to these digital assets due to their respective IP protections.

The following paragraphs will address the issues previously outlined, as they represent the fundamental challenges to the clear application of property rights to digital assets. What I will try to demonstrate is that the mere existence of intangible things under Czech civil law, existing within a category under civil law, does not automatically lead to the application of traditional property rights to digital assets and actually creates considerable legal uncertainty. These findings may be relevant to other legal systems, as the issues identified in the Czech legal framework, such as the question of whether digital assets may be both things and copyrighted works, may also arise in other jurisdictions. This being said, the purpose of this chapter is not to address and solve all the issues connected to the Czech Civil Code's property rights framework. The issues surrounding the concept of intangible things is much greater and includes more intangibles than those that are digital. This book only deals with the nature of digital assets and its scope is narrowed to finding and identifying the respective limitations.

[284] PETROV, Jan. § 979 [Věcná práva. Použitelnost ustanovení hlavy II.]. In: PETROV, Jan, VÝTISK, Michal, BERAN, Vladimír et al. *Občanský zákoník.* 2nd edition. Prague: C. H. Beck, 2023, marg. no. 13; ZVÁRA, Michael. § 979. In: ŠVESTKA, Jiří, DVOŘÁK, Jan el al. *Občanský zákoník: Komentář, Svazek III, (§ 976-1474).* [ASPI]. Wolters Kluwer [Accessed 2023-04-25]. ASPI_ID KO89_c2012CZ. Available at: www.aspi.cz. ISSN 2336-517X; SPÁČIL, Jiří. § 979 [Použití věcněprávních ustanovení na věci a práva]. In: SPÁČIL, Jiří, KRÁLÍK, Michal et al. Občanský zákoník III. Věcná práva (§ 976–1474). 2nd edition. Prague: C. H. Beck, 2021, p. 9, marg. no. 7.

[285] TÉGL, Petr. § 496. In: MELZER, Filip, TÉGL, Petr et al. *Občanský zákoník: velký komentář. Svazek III, § 419–653.* 2014, p. 238.

[286] TOMÍŠEK, Jan. Software jako věc v režimu nového občanského zákoníku. *Revue pro právo a technologie.* 2014, vol. 5, no. 9.

The first step of an analysis of whether digital assets can be the object of property rights is whether they can be classified as an (intangible) thing. Two steps are necessary in such an analysis. First, such digital assets must fulfil the definition of a thing under Section 489, Civil Code, which states that a thing is "*everything different from a person which serves the needs of people*". The adopted definition is inspired by the Austrian civil Code and appears identical, as Section 285 of ABGB defines a thing as (the similarly meaning) "*Alles, was von der Person unterschieden ist, und zum Gebrauche der Menschen dient.*"[287]

The definition actually includes more than just the two conditions referenced above, which I will address below. Moreover, once we determine whether a digital asset is a thing, we still need to solve whether it is an *intangible* thing. The Czech Civil Code recognizes two types of intangible things — rights whose nature allows this and other things without corporeal substance. This is also similar to Austrian law.[288] Accordingly, the final step is to determine which of these definitions applies.

4.1.1 The Requirements for an Object to be a Thing

As already noted, two requirements apply for something to be a thing under Article 489. Furthermore, one implicit condition is found in the Explanatory Memorandum, as widely repeated by legal commentators. This is that a thing must be capable of being an object of subjective property rights such as ownership.[289]

First, I will address the requirements explicitly specified by the Civil Code. These are 1) being different from a person and 2) to serve the needs of people. Although the latter requirement might be easily fulfilled, since digital assets are connected to economic (or another, e.g. sentimental) value to people, the former comes with one significant interpretational issue. Traditionally, the requirement to be "different from a person" included the condition not to be tied to the person in the sense of personal rights. Therefore, any expressions of a personal nature such as personal letters were considered not to be categorized as a thing. This may have consequences for those digital assets which carry a strong personal element, such as personal social media accounts, on which I will elaborate in the last part of this chapter. The personal element may present a challenge in other legal jurisdictions

[287] RAHMATIAN, Andreas. Debts, Money, Intellectual Property, Data and the Concept of Dematerialised Property. *Journal of Intellectual Property, Information Technology and Electronic Commerce Law.* 2020, vol. 11, no. 2, p. 187.

[288] PRADUROUX, Sabrina. Objects of Property Rights: Old and New. In: GRAZIADEI, Michele and SMITH, Lionel (eds.) *Comparative Property Law*. United Kingdom: Edward Elgar Publishing, 2017. ISBN 9781848447578, p. 55.

[289] Explanatory Memorandum. [online] [Accessed 2023-09-15]. Available at: http://obcanskyzakonik.justice.cz/images/pdf/Duvodova-zprava-NOZ-konsolidovana-verze.pdf, p. 118.
Section 496 paragraph 2, Civil Code.

as well. Szwajdler, for instance, argues that digital assets with a sentimental value should be excluded from inheritance due to their sentimental nature.[290]

Moreover, the condition of being "different from a person" is often referenced in connection to copyrighted works.[291] This is due to the fact that the historical intellectual property doctrine sees copyrighted works as "*springing from the personality rights of the creator*" where the emphasis is not given on the economic value, but on the protection of individual personality.[292] This led to the opinion that copyrighted works cannot by their very nature be a thing because as "springing from personality" they are, in fact, not different from a person.[293] Moreover, based on Section 9 paragraph 3 of the Czech Civil Code, which states that "*rights and obligations of a proprietary nature are only governed by the Civil Code unless they are not regulated by other laws*", the parallel application of both traditional property and intellectual property is excluded since copyrighted works are governed under the Copyright Act.[294]

Nevertheless, in past years, many legal commentators inclined to the interpretation that copyrighted works might be things in a legal sense, although with some limitations.[295] Furthermore, the Explanatory Memorandum itself references the objects of intellectual property rights as examples of what can be considered a thing under the Czech Civil Code.[296] Additionally, one possible interpretation is that copyrighted works (and other intangible things) are simply "*things without property rights*".[297]

However, this again begs the question of why they should be recognised as things in the first place. A possible answer is that although property rights might not apply, numerous provisions still require something to be a thing.[298] For instance, this

[290] SZWAJDLER, Paweł. "Digital assets and inheritance law: How to create fundamental principles of digital succession system?" Online. *International journal of law and information technology*. 2023, vol. 31, no. 2, p. 157.

[291] KOUKAL, Pavel. § 489 [Pojem věci v právním smyslu]. In: LAVICKÝ, Petr et al. *Občanský zákoník I. Obecná část (§ 1–654).* 2nd edition. Prague: C. H. Beck, 2022, p. 1494, marg. no. 15.

[292] MACQUEEN, Hector, Charlotte WAELDE, Graeme LAURIE and Abbe BROWN. *Contemporary Intellectual Property.* 2nd. Oxford University Press, 2011. ISBN 978-0-19-957532-9, p. 44.

[293] BEZOUŠKA, Petr. § 1310 [Zástava]. In: SPÁČIL, Jiří, KRÁLÍK, Michal et al. *Občanský zákoník III. Věcná práva (§ 976–1474).* 2nd edition. Prague: C. H. Beck, 2021, p. 1245–1246, marg. no. 2.

[294] TOMÍŠEK, Jan. Software jako věc v režimu nového občanského zákoníku. *Revue pro právo a technologie.* 2014, vol. 5, no. 9, p. 199.

[295] For instance, KOUKAL, Pavel. § 496 [Věci hmotné a nehmotné]. In: LAVICKÝ, Petr et al. *Občanský zákoník I. Obecná část (§ 1–654).* 2nd ediiton. Prague: C. H. Beck, 2022, p. 1531, marg. no. 23. or SVOBODA, Karel. § 489. In: ŠVESTKA, Jiří et al. *Občanský zákoník: Komentář, Svazek I, (§ 1–654).* [Systém ASPI]. Wolters Kluwer [Accessed 2023-04-25]. ASPI_ID KO89_a2012CZ. Available at: www.aspi.cz.

[296] Explanatory Memorandum. [online] [Accessed 2023-09-15]. Available at: http://obcanskyzakonik.justice.cz/images/pdf/Duvodova-zprava-NOZ-konsolidovana-verze.pdf, p. 117.

[297] TELEC, Ivo. Držba informací. *Právní rozhledy*, 2014, vol. 4, p. 115–121; TELEC, Ivo. Nový občanský zákoník ve společnosti sítí. *Bulletin advokacie.* [online] 17. 6. 2015. [Accessed 2023-10-31]. Available at: http://www.bulletin-advokacie.cz/novy-obcansky-zakonik-ve-spolecnosti-siti.

[298] TOMÍŠEK, Jan. Software jako věc v režimu nového občanského zákoníku. *Revue pro právo a technologie.* 2014, vol. 5, no. 9, p. 199.

might be the case of intangible things being used as a deposit or simply belonging to one's property.

Furthermore, a court recently embraced the broad category of a thing for something otherwise protected by copyright law. In a case when a company's database was copied by a former employee, a Czech criminal court concluded not only that a database is an intangible thing according to the Czech Civil Code, but also that the company was the owner of this database.[299] Despite this interpretation coming via a criminal court, it is still relevant to the debate because the conclusions were derived from the court's interpretation of the Civil Code. Unfortunately, the judgement only offers this conclusion without providing any additional analysis. Moreover, it appears that the court combined the database rights stemming from copyright law and the traditional property framework, since the court also stated that because the company was the owner of the database, it may decide on its "*reproduction by copying or export to another format.*"[300] This is probably due to the fact that the judgment was delivered by a criminal court and not a civil court. In the end, the judgement on the one hand shows how the broad category of things is recognized, and on the other hand, it also indicates how a parallel protection with intellectual property in some cases might be confusing. Thus, we can only conclude that for the purposes of criminal law, the concept of a thing may be expanded to a copyright work; however, this does not automatically mean the same would apply in a civil law matter. Yet, the case serves as an example that the broad category of a thing may have legal consequences outside of the scope of property rights.

In my view, a middle ground of interpretation can be found when it comes to copyrighted works. The doctrine was built for a world without technology and may be applicable to traditional works of art. However, the idea of a "springing of personality" is hardly applicable to software or databases, as these are not usually created by some creative process. In contrast, traditional copyrighted works such as poems or visual art are. Consequently, I would argue that that the condition of "being different from a person" should be interpreted strictly, and that it should only apply in cases where a clear "springing of personality" is found, and by default to all works that fall under the category of copyrighted works.

The question still remains of the legal consequences for copyrighted works if they are, at the same time, a thing. This could potentially mean one person has property rights such as ownership in the same object to which another person holds a copyright. However, this is a distinct legal issue from the initial consideration of whether an object should be classified as a thing.

What might be an issue in the case of digital assets is the implicit condition of being an object of subjective property rights such as ownership. The Explanatory

[299] Judgement of the Czech Supreme Court, 5 Tdo 1085/2017 from 13. 12. 2017.

[300] Ibid, paragraph 36.

Memorandum explains this condition to be an expression of the fact that things are "controllable"[301] and may be "appropriated."[302]

However, this condition is not something that can be typically fulfilled by intangible objects. Moreover, we can encounter strong opinions that intangible things cannot be the object of subjective property rights, as one cannot have absolute legal dominion over intangible things.[303] This conviction also seems to lead to a circular definition, because 1) for something to be thing, it must be possible for it to be an object of subjective property rights and 2) only a thing may be an object of property rights.

On the other hand, this requirement for things to be controllable may simply mean that intangible things allow for legal control instead of physical control.[304] This interpretation offers a possibility for digital assets to be at least controllable and thus partially fulfil the condition for being the object of subjective property rights (the only issue would be that legal control would be in the hands of service providers per their terms and conditions).

The requirement for a thing to be capable of being an object of subjective property rights could also be seen as a requirement to prove an object's proprietary quality.[305] This requirement can be understood as meaning that the object of property rights must be clearly and precisely defined within obvious boundaries.[306] Moreover, the condition may be interpreted through the criteria for a physical object, which must be, e.g., capable of being an object of possession.[307] This interpretation can allow at least for some digital assets, such as cryptoassets, to fulfil the condition of being an object of subjective property rights. However, with others, such as those digital assets whose use is limited by contractual terms, the condition to be capable of being an object of possession might be hard to fulfil.

In the end, it appears that the system of property rights was created solely with tangible objects in mind, while at the same time, legislators sought to create a novel broad category of things. In this sense Czech regulation appears flawed, as it achieved its goal only half-way. Looking at the Austrian civil code, which served as an inspiration for the Czech civil code, the approach is not that different. The

---

301 Explanatory Memorandum. [online] [Accessed 2023-09-15]. Available at: http://obcanskyzakonik.justice.cz/images/pdf/Duvodova-zprava-NOZ-konsolidovana-verze.pdf, p. 118.

302 Ibid.

303 KOUKAL, Pavel. § 496 [Věci hmotné a nehmotné]. In: LAVICKÝ, Petr et al. *Občanský zákoník I. Obecná část (§ 1–654).* 2nd edition. Prague: C. H. Beck, 2022, p. 1529, marg. no. 13; SPÁČIL, Jiří, KRÁLÍK, Michal. § 1040 [Žaloba na vydání věci (reivindikace)]. In: SPÁČIL, Jiří, KRÁLÍK, Michal et al. *Občanský zákoník III. Věcná práva (§ 976–1474).* 2nd edition. Prague: C. H. Beck, 2021, p. 234–236, marg. no. 42–44.

304 KOUKAL, Pavel. § 496 [Věci hmotné a nehmotné]. In: LAVICKÝ, Petr et al. *Občanský zákoník I. Obecná část (§ 1–654).* 2nd edition. Prague: C. H. Beck, 2022, p. 1529, marg. no. 9.

305 RAHMATIAN, Andreas. Debts, Money, Intellectual Property, Data and the Concept of Dematerialised Property. *Journal of Intellectual Property, Information Technology and Electronic Commerce Law.* 2020, vol. 11, no. 2, p. 192.

306 Ibid.

307 Ibid., p. 193.

applicability of property rights for incorporeal things under the ABGB is also limited, as the law was primarily meant for the protection of tangible things.[308]

In summary, the definition of things under Article 489, Czech Civil Code cannot be easily applied to everything that is colloquially considered to be a digital asset. Even though legislators intended to have a broad category of a thing, the definition coupled with the implicit condition from the Explanatory Memorandum creates many interpretational obstacles for the actual application on digital assets. This does not mean that such an interpretation is impossible. In my opinion, the broad category of a thing should be the leading interpretational principle and should prevail, since it was legislators' intent and offers flexibility for the digital age. However, the actual interpretation is fully at the discretion of the courts, which will have more possibilities to choose from, and will have to opt for one interpretation out of many possibilities. Thus, here, unclear laws represent a limit to the application of digital assets concepts.

4.1.2 Rights or Things without. Corporeal Substance?

Some digital assets are provided on the basis of a contractual relationship between a service provider and a user. This opens up the question of whether the object of property rights, i.e. a thing, is the rights stemming from the given contract or the actual digital object (such as, for example, an account). Traditionally, intangible things in Roman law were not all incorporeal things, but rights.[309] The Roman law categorization is partly present in the Czech Civil Code, according to which intangible things are "*rights whose nature allows it and other things without corporeal substance*." Rights whose nature allows it are understood as those that have economic value, are transferable, and their nature is proprietary, such as industrial rights or an author's economic rights.[310] As result, in order to determine the object of property rights, it must be assessed whether the rights derive from a contract, the actual given digital asset, or both.

Legal literature lists many examples of intangible things under the Czech Civil Code. The table below lists examples of what the commentaries to the Czech Civil Code specifically recognize as intangible things in a legal sense:

- databases[311]

[308] PRADUROUX, Sabrina. Objects of Property Rights: Old and New. In: GRAZIADEI, Michele and SMITH, Lionel (eds.) *Comparative Property Law*. United Kingdom: Edward Elgar Publishing, 2017. ISBN 9781848447578, p. 61.

[309] PAŁKA, Przemysław. Virtual Property — Towards a General Theory. 2017, p. 149; PRADUROUX, Sabrina. Objects of property rights: old and new. In: GRAZIADEI, Michele and SMITH, Lionel (eds.) *Comparative Property Law*. United Kingdom: Edward Elgar Publishing, 2017. ISBN 9781848447578, pp. 57–58.

[310] HUBKOVÁ, Pavlína. § 496 [Věci hmotné a nehmotné]. In: PETROV, Jan, VÝTISK, Michal, BERAN, Vladimír et al. Občanský zákoník. 2nd edition. Prague: C. H. Beck, 2023, marg. no. 7.

[311] KOUKAL, Pavel. § 496 [Věci hmotné a nehmotné]. In: LAVICKÝ, Petr et al. *Občanský zákoník I. Obecná část (§ 1–654)*. 2nd edition. Prague: C. H. Beck, 2022, p. 1531, marg. no. 22.

- business names[312]
- information, if having economic value[313]
- know-how[314]
- domain names[315]
- trademarks[316]
- software[317]
- trade secrets[318]
- business shares[319]

This means that civil law commentators are actually inclining towards a wide interpretation when it comes to intangible things. We may thus observe a trend that the broad definition of a thing opens the interpretational possibility of considering an intangible object to be a thing in a legal sense.

However, it is also important to stress that the respective commentaries do not offer any analysis or explanation as to why these examples are in fact intangible things. Moreover, views on the nature of rights versus things without corporeal substance are also not united. Opinions can be found that domain names and databases are things without corporal nature and therefore not rights.[320] But at the same time, a line of argumentation exists that a sword in a video game is not a thing, whereas the obligation from the contact to the game account is deemed a thing.[321] The problem is that both a domain name and a sword in a video game are colloquially considered digital assets and both are typically based

312 Judgement of the Czech Supreme Court NS 31 Cdo 3375/2015

313 SVOBODA, Karel. § 496. In: ŠVESTKA, Jiří et al. *Občanský zákoník: Komentář, Svazek I, (§ 1–654).* [Systém ASPI]. Wolters Kluwer [Accessed 2023-04-25]. ASPI_ID KO89_a2012CZ. Available at: www.aspi.cz.

314 KOUKAL, Pavel. § 496 [Věci hmotné a nehmotné]. In: LAVICKÝ, Petr et al. *Občanský zákoník I. Obecná část (§ 1–654).* 2nd edition. Prague: C. H. Beck, 2022, p. 1531, marg. no. 22.

315 PETROV, Jan. § 979 [Věcná práva. Použitelnost ustanovení hlavy II.]. In: PETROV, Jan, VÝTISK, Michal, BERAN, Vladimír et al. *Občanský zákoník.* 2nd edition. Prague: C. H. Beck, 2022, marg. no. 22.

316 ZVÁRA, Michael. § 979 In: ŠVESTKA, Jiří, DVOŘÁK, Jan et al. *Občanský zákoník: Komentář, Svazek III, (§ 976–1474).* [ASPI]. Wolters Kluwer [Accessed 2023-04-25]. ASPI_ID KO89_c2012CZ. Available at: www.aspi.cz.

317 Ibid.

318 SMOLKOVÁ, Michaela. § 1011 [Předmět vlastnického práva]. In: PETROV, Jan, VÝTISK, Michal, BERAN, Vladimír et al. *Občanský zákoník.* 2nd edition. Prague: C. H. Beck, 2023.

319 Ibid.

320 TELEC, Ivo. Nový občanský zákoník ve společnosti sítí. *Bulletin advokacie.* [online] 17. 6. 2015. [Accessed 2023-10-31]. Available from: http://www.bulletin-advokacie.cz/novy-obcansky-zakonik-ve-spolecnosti-siti; ZVÁRA, Michael. § 979 In: ŠVESTKA, Jiří, DVOŘÁK, Jan el al. *Občanský zákoník: Komentář, Svazek III, (§ 976–1474).* [ASPI]. Wolters Kluwer [Accessed 2023-04-25]. ASPI_ID KO89_c2012CZ. Available at: www.aspi.cz; KOUKAL, Pavel. § 496 [Věci hmotné a nehmotné]. In: LAVICKÝ, Petr et al. *Občanský zákoník I. Obecná část (§ 1–654).* 2nd edition. Prague: C. H. Beck, 2022, p. 1531, marg. no. 22.

321 POLČÁK, Radim. Protiprávní jednání a škoda online. *Bulletin advokacie*. 2021, no. 6, p. 17.

on contractual relationships. Consequently, no valid reason exists for this inconsistent treatment.

Moreover, arguments have also been heard that the rights stemming from contracts are not things because they cannot be transferred and only a change of the subject of the contract is possible. But that is not a transfer; just the assignment of a contract.[322] This opinion was recently upheld via two decisions of the Czech Supreme Court.[323] In the first decision, the court stated that if the respective rights do not allow for a permanent or repeated exercise (which is the case of claims and other relative property rights), their nature does not allow for them to be intangible things.[324] In the second decision, the court confirmed the previous findings and strictly concluded that none of the relative property rights were intangible things under both Section 496 and Section 797 of the Czech Civil Code.[325]

I concur with this position to the point that it solves the inconsistency issue concerning the interpretation of digital assets. Through this strict interpretation, the courts ultimately concluded that contractual relations are not things. Applied to digital assets, this approach overcomes the dual interpretation concerning the object of property rights. If we eliminate contractual relations between users and the service providers, we can conclude that a thing is an exact digital asset, for example an in-game object.

4.2 Digital Assets as the Component of a Thing and the Accessory to a Thing

Other relevant provisions of the Czech Civil Code are those detailing the so-called component of a thing and accessory to a thing. The difference between them is that an accessory may be separated from a thing without devaluing its value.[326] Whether something is a component is determined based on objective criteria. These criteria mean that a component is what the wider public considers to be a component given its factual and legal characteristics as opposed to what an individual might decide.[327] The common example of a component of a thing is a car vehicle technical certificate[328], while an accessory can be an external DVD

322 HUBKOVÁ, Pavlína. § 496 [Věci hmotné a nehmotné]. In: PETROV, Jan, VÝTISK, Michal, BERAN, Vladimír et al. Občanský zákoník. 2nd edition. Prague: C. H. Beck, 2023, marg. no. 7.

323 Judgement of the Czech Supreme Court, 23 Cdo 3320/2020 from 30 August 2021, and Judgement of the Czech Supreme Court, 33 Cdo 3720/2020 from 25 November 2021.

324 Judgement of the Czech Supreme Court, 23 Cdo 3320/2020 from 30 August 2021.

325 Judgement of the Czech Supreme Court, 33 Cdo 3720/2020 from 25 November 2021.

326 Section 505 and 510, Czech Civil Code.

327 SVOBODA, Karel. § 505. In: ŠVESTKA, Jiří et al. *Občanský zákoník: Komentář, Svazek I, (§ 1–654).* [Systém ASPI]. Wolters Kluwer [Accessed 2023-04-25]. ASPI_ID KO89_a2012CZ. Available at: www.aspi.cz.

328 Judgement of the Czech Supreme Court from 11 March 2007, 21 Cdo 694/2006.

player for a computer.[329] It also important to note that an accessory is a separate autonomous thing while a component is a thing, but also cannot exist on its own.

These two institutes are relevant to the classification of digital assets because they can help us conceptualize the exact nature of a thing and how the complex data structure of digital assets can be handled. For example, many digital assets come in a form to which one needs certain access information, be it an account with a password or a private wallet. This access information, on its own, might also be categorized as an intangible thing. The question is, are they components or accessories? As stems from the nature of these institutes, the answers depend on how much the primary thing (e.g. a social media account or cryptoassets) would be devalued without such access information. And this devaluation might potentially differ based on the nature of each individual asset.

It is also important to analyse what exactly is meant by a primary thing being devalued. I would argue that the subjective and objective aspects of value apply when it comes to access information to digital assets. By objective, I mean whether digital assets are actually deprived of their value without such access information. For example, the price for a Bitcoin will remain the same irrespective of whether someone possesses the given private key. Conversely, the subjective value lies with the user and their ability to derive benefit from the value. Here, without the access information, the digital assets are completely useless to the user because they cannot actually derive any benefit from or control them. Legal literature argues that a thing is devalued once "*an objectively accepted standard of functional use or legal control of a thing is fundamentally disrupted.*"[330] Based on the aforementioned, I would argue that subjective value is what is important and thus that access information is a component more than an accessory.

4.3 The Extent of Applicability of Property Rights

As noted in the introduction to this chapter, the simple categorization of digital assets as intangible things does not automatically mean that these assets benefit from property rights. The wording of Section 979 limits the application of property rights to intangible things. Moreover, we come across opinions that intangible things cannot be the object of property law ownership, as ownership can only be attached to tangible things.[331]

[329] SVOBODA, Karel. § 510. In: ŠVESTKA, Jiří et al. *Občanský zákoník: Komentář, Svazek I, (§ 1–654).* [Systém ASPI]. Wolters Kluwer [Accessed 2023-04-25]. ASPI_ID KO89_a2012CZ. Available at: www.aspi.cz.

[330] Ibid.

[331] KOUKAL, Pavel. § 496 [Věci hmotné a nehmotné]. In: LAVICKÝ, Petr et al. *Občanský zákoník I. Obecná část (§ 1–654).* 2nd edition. Prague: C. H. Beck, 2022, p. 1529, marg. no. 13; TÉGL, Petr. § 496. In: MELZER, Filip, TÉGL, Petr et al. *Občanský zákoník: velký komentář. Svazek III, § 419–653.* 2014, p. 243.

Thus, only possession of intangible things is possible.[332] In the following subchapters I will seek to explore the possibilities of applying property rights to digital assets with an emphasis on ownership. What this will hopefully demonstrate is that the *numerus clausus* of Czech property rights is indeed not suitable for digital assets. Moreover, I will argue that since ownership to a digital asset cannot be acquired, we also cannot apply other property rights.

Czech law recognizes the following property rights as its *numerus clausus*:

- Ownership (including co-ownership)
- The right of superficies
- Easements
- Real burdens
- Pledges
- Retention rights

It is important to emphasize that under Czech law, similarly to German law, *numerus clausus* is strictly prescribed by the law, as opposed to the French or Spanish systems.[333] Therefore, only legislator can create new property rights. In the following paragraphs, I will offer considerations on the difficulties of applying *numerus clausus* principles to digital assets. However, given the broadness of this subject, I will primarily focus on ownership.

The first question is which of these property rights could apply when it comes to digital assets. At first glance, it is evident that we can eliminate the right to superficies, as this property right is meant for cases when one person builds a construction on land owned by another. Yes, it might conceivably be of interest to explore the right of superficies in connection to virtual reality and the metaverse, if we imagine a virtual intangible immovable thing such as virtual land in a game. However, this would mean that some users would have to have ownership rights to virtual land and such virtual land would have to be considered as immovable.

Similarly, we can exclude real burdens. Under Czech civil law, only things registered in the public register (like immovables) can be encumbered with a real burden.[334] Since presently no digital assets are being registered (perhaps with the exception of domain names, and even those do not have a public registry), it is not necessary to continue with a consideration of the application of the provision on real burdens.

Comparatively, conclusions for the application of easements are not as straightforward. Easements are defined as the right of a person to use a thing in someone else's ownership, whereby the owner of a thing needs to abstain from using such

[332] TÉGL, Petr. § 496. In: MELZER, Filip, TÉGL, Petr et al. *Občanský zákoník: velký komentář. Svazek III, § 419–653*. 2014, p. 243.

[333] AKKERMANS, Bram. The Numerus Clausus of Property Rights. In: GRAZIADEI, Michele and SMITH, Lionel (eds.) *Comparative Property Law*. United Kingdom: Edward Elgar Publishing, 2017. ISBN 9781848447578, pp. 101–103.

[334] Section 1303, Czech Civil Code.

a thing.[335] Therefore, in theory, we can come to the conclusion that a digital asset might be capable of being exactly that thing from whose usage the owner needs to abstain. Here, I can think of cases when the owner is the service provider who permits the user to have an easement over a digital asset. However, there are two issues with this consideration. First, why would the service provider do that? I can only think of cases when such a right of easement would be mandatory by law (which it is not). Second, we need a thing that is owned by someone in the first place. Thus, the service provider would have to be the owner of the given digital assets.

For something to be a pledge, it needs to be a tradeable thing. The Czech Civil Code does not offer a definition of "tradeable". An evident consensus, however, suggests that it means that the given thing has a monetary value that may satisfy the respective debt.[336] Conversely, tradeable does not mean that the thing must be transferable.[337] As a result, the fact that digital assets might not always be transferable does not mean that they cannot be the object of a pledge, as long as their monetary value can be estimated. I will not delve here into the theory behind pledges over all sorts of intangible things and whether they are possible, as that would be outside of the scope of this work. I will only stress that the existence of a debtor's ownership over the object of a pledge is required. This right might be acquired in the future[338], however; but a thing must exist for which someone has ownership rights.

A retention right might also be possible, however, via a slightly different mechanism. Due to the technical realities, the service provider will be a person capable of actually retaining a thing if needed. Therefore, in order to apply retention rights effectively, we would need the user to be the "owner" of the digital assets to which the service provider claims retention. I can think of cryptoassets being a primary example where this could work. Moreover, I purposely put the "owner" of the given digital assets into quotation marks, because the law does not explicitly state that the person must be an owner of the retained thing. The law only indirectly notes that retention is connected to "someone else's thing"[339] which might lead to an assumption of ownership. However, retention fulfils its purpose even without that. We only need a thing that has value. So as long as digital assets are a "thing", I do not see any reason why retention cannot apply even if the user would not be owner.

The above analysis underscores that the crucial question is **whether we can establish ownership over digital assets.** This is because first, an object being owned by someone is the prerequisite for the application of certain property rights (such as easements or pledges).

---

[335] Section 1257, Czech Civil Code.

[336] BEZOUŠKA, Petr. § 1310 [Zástava]. In: SPÁČIL, Jiří, KRÁLÍK, Michal et al. *Občanský zákoník III. Věcná práva (§ 976–1474)*. 2nd edition. Prague: C. H. Beck, 2021, p. 1246, marg. č. 8; HAMPL, Ondřej. § 1310 [Zástava]. In: PETROV, Jan, VÝTISK, Michal, BERAN, Vladimír et al. *Občanský zákoník*. 2nd edition. Prague: C. H. Beck, 2023, marg. no. 4–5.

[337] Ibid.

[338] Section 1310, paragraph 2, Czech Civil Code.

[339] Section 1396, Czech Civil Code.

Furthermore, ownership has another important consequence, namely the possibility to file proprietary claims such as *rei vindicatio*.[340] However, multiple issues exist with reivindication under Czech property law. First, the theory recognizes that only individually determined tangible things may be reivindicated and as a result, a *rei vindicatio* claim cannot be used for intangible things. [341] This is strengthened by the condition that the plaintiff must "*either distinguish his thing from the others or, if not possible, it must be determined that the plaintiff has ownership over the thing*".[342] Second, only an owner or qualified possessor may make use of such a claim.[343] Both of these conditions may be an obstacle in practice, because digital assets are usually not tangible or individually determined things. Thirdly, the claimant must prove the legal basis (e.g. a contract) on which they acquired ownership.[344] This brings us back again to the necessity to determine how a person may acquire the ownership of digital assets.

Three requirements for ownership must be met. First, we need an object capable of being an object of ownership. This object must be a thing. The considerations as to whether digital assets might be a thing were already discussed in previous subchapters. Second, we need a subject to be the owner. In cyberspace, this would typically either be a service provider or the user. Thirdly, we need to assign ownership to one of these two entities. Thus, we need a legal basis on which one or the other becomes the owner. Below, I will address whether and how the ownership of digital assets can be established.

4.3.1 How Can Ownership in Digital Assets be Acquired?

Calls for the ownership of digital assets are arguably justified. A common notorious example is the legal consequences of buying a physical copy of an otherwise intangible medium (such as a book). When one buys a physical copy, one may do anything with it because they own this copy. But when a buyer only receives a license to an intangible medium, the possibilities of what one can do are significantly limited. Suddenly, one cannot simply borrow or sell it. Moreover, at the moment the service

[340] Whether a *rei vindicatio* claim can be used to recover digital data was an issue recently addressed by the Dutch Commercial Court in a case where the plaintiff needed to recover digital documents, see Judgement of the Netherlands Commercial Court from 21 April 2023, NCC 22/018.

[341] DOBROVOLNÁ, Eva. § 1040 [Reivindikační žaloba]. In: PETROV, Jan, VÝTISK, Michal, BERAN, Vladimír et al. *Občanský zákoník.* 2nd edition. Prague: C. H. Beck, 2023, marg. no. 3; SPÁČIL, Jiří, KRÁLÍK, Michal. § 1040 [Žaloba na vydání věci (reivindikace)]. In: SPÁČIL, Jiří, KRÁLÍK, Michal et al. *Občanský zákoník III. Věcná práva (§ 976–1474).* 2nd edition. Prague: C. H. Beck, 2021, p. 234–236, marg. no. 42–44.

[342] Section 1041 Czech Civil Code.

[343] Ibid., marg. no. 6.

[344] SPÁČIL, Jiří, KRÁLÍK, Michal. § 1040 [Žaloba na vydání věci (reivindikace)]. In: SPÁČIL, Jiří, KRÁLÍK, Michal et al. *Občanský zákoník III. Věcná práva (§ 976–1474).* 2nd edition. Prague: C. H. Beck, 2021, p. 228, marg. no. 9.

provider decides to terminate that user's access to the purchase, even usage is negated.[345] This disparity between ownership in the physical world and cyberspace has led to a vast body of literature arguing in favour of applying a traditional property law framework in the online world.

Ownership is understood differently across various legal systems. However, the basis of the concept remains the same — a legal relationship between persons with regards to what the law recognizes as things.[346] As a result, the nature of the object of ownership will vary in common and civil law systems, and even among distinct jurisdictions within the civil law system. However, some features are universal. For example, Swinnen notes that ownership has generally multiple default rules such as:

- the owner may exercise an *orga omnes* right
- they may reivindicate the object of the ownership right
- ownership passes after the owner's death, or
- the owner may encumber the thing[347]

Similarly, a bundle of rights is typically associated with ownership, for example the right of control, right of disposal, or the right of exclusion. Additionally, ownership rights lay down the legal relationship between people — i.e. if one person owns something, they have the control over it and others are limited in the disposition with such a thing.[348] This is why the ownership concept is so powerful. One simply has almost unlimited power to decide what they can do with what they own. This may ultimately mean that ownership rights are what regulates influence over resources.[349] But in the end, when applying an ownership regime, one must examine the respective legal system and determine potential applicability. The fact that something can be an object of ownership in one jurisdiction does not mean this is the case in another. It also means that the manner in which one can acquire ownership differs with each legal system. Moreover, as noted in Chapter 2, contract law cannot itself establish ownership.[350]

The Czech Civil Code recognizes the following acquisitions of ownership[351]:

- Appropriation
- Discovery

---

345 PERZANOWSKI, Aaron a Jason M SCHULTZ. *The End of Ownership: Personal Property in the Digital Eaconomy.* Cambridge: The MIT Press, 2016. ISBN 0-262-33596-4, p. 2.

346 RAHMATIAN, Andreas. Debts, Money, Intellectual Property, Data and the Concept of Dematerialised Property. *Journal of Intellectual Property, Information Technology and Electronic Commerce Law.* 2020, vol. 11, no. 2, p. 188.

347 SWINNEN, Koen. Ownership of Data: Four Recommendations for Future Research. *Journal of Law, Property, and Society*, vol. 5, no. 3, p. 150.

348 PERZANOWSKI, Aaron a Jason M SCHULTZ. *The End of Ownership: Personal Property in the Digital Eaconomy.* Cambridge: The MIT Press, 2016. ISBN 0-262-33596-4, p. 22.

349 FAIRFIELD, Joshua. *Owned: Property, Privacy, and the New Digital Serfdom.* Cambridge: Cambridge University Press, 2017, p. 13.

350 HUMMEL, Patrik, Matthias BRAUN a Peter DABROCK. Own Data? Ethical Reflections on Data Ownership. *Philosophy & Technology*. 2021, vol. 34, no. 3, p. 548.

351 Section 1045, Czech Civil Code, and following.

- Natural accession, such as alluvium
- Artificial accession, such as processing or mixing
- Acquisitive prescription (addressed in the following chapter)

Through examining this list, it is evident that the system of acquisition was made for the physical world. Moreover, it is also wholly evident that the specific listed cases are a "relic" from centuries ago.

Those concepts that might apply are appropriation and processing. However, processing has the condition that it only applies to things that do not belong to a person. Thus, even if agreed that what is being processed is data (and again, this data would have been someone's property, which is not something the theory generally allows for), the analogical use of this institute appears to be incredibly forced, and if one actually processed its own source / data, it would not apply. The same goes for appropriation. This institute was once again built for the physical world. How could one appropriate something in cyberspace? I can imagine cases in the metaverse where it would be possible due to its immersive nature. It is a bit of a stretch, but I could also see this possibility with social media accounts, if an account was truly abandoned and someone else simply appropriated it (and the terms and conditions allowed it). But that is as far as I can go.

The logical conclusion would be that a service provider or a user becomes the owner upon the moment of creation of a new thing. This, for example, is the way that Dutch law recognizes the acquisition of ownership.[352] The creation of a new thing is also listed as a way of acquisition under Czech property law in academic texts.[353] Yet, the creation of a new thing is absent from the current text of the Czech civil code. This opens up the question of whether such a method is even possible if not explicitly recognized by the law given the cogent nature of property rights.

Accordingly, it appears that none of the available provisions are applicable for many digital assets. For example, how to apply provisions on the creation of social media accounts? Registration does not fit any concept. What about generating AI work? Writing prompts again does not fit. Uploading a picture in order to create NFT is the same. This process of creation of digital assets is a broad spectrum of actions. The law has had centuries to perfect its provisions on the physical world, and we encounter very detailed provisions concerning land. But nothing to tackle cyberspace. Moreover, this means that ownership is not a right one transfers when transferring digital assets due to the *nemo dat quod non habet* principle.

The above does not mean that digital assets cannot be property, as the category of property is slightly broader. It also does not mean that in different jurisdictions digital assets can be owned. However, examining how ownership is acquired under Czech law, I simply do not see how this is possible.

---

352 Judgement of the Netherlands Commercial Court from 21 April 2023, NCC 22/018, paragraph 4.36.

353 DVOŘÁK, Jan, Jiří ŠVESTKA et al. *Občanské právo hmotné* 3. Praha: Wolters Kluwer, 2015. ISBN 978-80-7478-935-9, p. 48.

To sum up, property rights are a highly complex system with many categories under which we seek to categorise digital assets. In the end, we face layers and layers of issues connected to the complicated structure of cyberspace. To establish ownership, we first must identify the respective layer. In the case of digital assets, the relevant layer should either be an account (as digital assets often depend on them) or the actual digital assets (which we access through accounts).

4.4 The Concept of Control

Since digital assets are intangible by their nature, it is often hard to apply traditional property rights, especially because of the lack of a physical aspect. This is well demonstrated by the limitations on the application of property rights on intangible things under Czech civil law. This is also the reason why digital assets are often connected to the concept of control. For example, UNIDROIT sees control as a defining feature for digital assets.[354] Furthermore, the UK Law Commission recently proposed applying the concept of control as an alternative to the possession of digital assets, as it is better suited to their nature as opposed to possession, which is more suited to tangible objects.[355] In the Commission's view, control still allows for some basic functionalities of property law such as exclusion or the permission of others.[356] The concept of control has thus been addressed by both UNIDROIT and the UK Law Commission, and will be further examined in this paper in order to determine whether it may be a useful interpretational clue for the concept of possession. Because control is not a property right under Czech law, and arguably, under any civil law jurisdiction, it should first be analysed whether it is possible to interpret control as possession, since the category of possession inherently requires control.[357]

As noted, control is not a legal concept or legal category, and at present, its understanding stems purely from the functioning of digital assets — and the understanding of this concept slightly differs. Therefore, it is important to examine what exactly is meant by control and how this concept is helpful with the application of property rights or possession to digital assets.

For instance, UNIDROIT defines control as:

[354] UNIDROIT. Digital Assets and Private Law. [online] April 2023 [Accessed 2023-07-20]. Available at: https://www.unidroit.org/wp-content/uploads/2023/04/C.D.-102-6-Principles-on-Digital-Assets-and-Private-Law.pdf, p. 11.

[355] UK LAW COMMISSION. Digital Asset: Final Report. [online] 27. 6. 2023 [Accessed 2024-05-20]. Available at: https://cloud-platform-e218f50a4812967ba1215eaecede923f.s3.amazonaws.com/uploads/sites/30/2023/06/Final-digital-assets-report-FOR-WEBSITE-2.pdf, p. 40; UK LAW COMMISSION. Digital Assets Consultation Paper. [online] 28. 7. 2022 [Accessed 2024-05-20]. Available at: https://cloud-platform-e218f50a4812967ba1215eaecede923f.s3.amazonaws.com/uploads/sites/30/2022/07/Digital-Assets-Consultation-Paper-Law-Commission-1.pdf, p. 212.

[356] Ibid., p. 84.

[357] EMERICH, Yaell. Possession. In: GRAZIADEI, Michele and SMITH, Lionel (eds.) *Comparative Property Law.* United Kingdom: Edward Elgar Publishing, 2017. ISBN 9781848447578.

"*(1) A person has 'control' of a digital asset if:*

(a) subject to paragraphs (2) and (3), the digital asset, or the relevant protocol or system, confers on that person:

(i) the exclusive ability to prevent others from obtaining substantially all of the benefit from the digital asset;

(ii) the ability to obtain substantially all of the benefit from the digital asset; and

(iii) the exclusive ability to transfer the abilities in sub-paragraphs (a)(i), (a)(ii) and (a)(iii) to another person; and

(b) the digital asset, or the relevant protocols or system, allows that person to identify itself as having the abilities set out in sub-paragraph (a)."[358]

The definition sees control as a factual concept while at the same time, it recognizes that legal consequences apply to control, such as it is inherently linked to property rights.[359] What this means is that control equals power and dominium over digital assets but not anything that is connected to the physical aspects of possession of tangible things.[360] This definition may have its shortcomings (which is mostly that many digital assets such as in-game objects or accounts will not fulfil it); however, what we can observe is that it tries to define control through the lens of possession (while explicitly claiming that control does not equal possession[361]). Requirements such as exclusivity or taking the respective benefits are well known under traditional property rights.

The UK law Commission did not directly define what control is. However, they nonetheless outlined what is to be understood under the concept. This is the ability to exclude or permit access to the third category of things, or to put it to the uses of which it is capable.[362] Thus, the understanding is not different from UNIDROIT, although it is simplified. The major difference from UNIDROIT is that they do not believe control should be a defining feature of digital assets.[363]

The question is whether the concept of control may be used to interpret the concept of possession. The meaning of possession will differ from jurisdiction to jurisdiction. Despite differences in the concept of possession across many jurisdictions, some universal effects apply to possession, such as a legal protection against

358 Principle 6 of Principles on Digital Assets and Private Law.

359 UNIDROIT. Digital Assets and Private Law. [online] April 2023 [Accessed 2023-07-20]. Available at: https://www.unidroit.org/wp-content/uploads/2023/04/C.D.-102-6-Principles-on-Digital-Assets-and-Private-Law.pdf, p. 52.

360 Ibid.

361 Ibid., p. 2.

362 UK LAW COMMISSION. Digital Asset: Final Report. [online] 27. 6. 2023 [Accessed 2024-05-20]. Available at: https://cloud-platform-e218f50a4812967ba1215eaecede923f.s3.amazonaws.com/uploads/sites/30/2023/06/Final-digital-assets-report-FOR-WEBSITE-2.pdf, pp. 24–25; 84.

363 UK LAW COMMISSION. Digital Asset: Final Report. [online] 27. 6. 2023 [Accessed 2024-05-20]. Available at: https://cloud-platform-e218f50a4812967ba1215eaecede923f.s3.amazonaws.com/uploads/sites/30/2023/06/Final-digital-assets-report-FOR-WEBSITE-2.pdf, p. 24.

other parties.[364] Moreover, under civil law, possession is typically not considered a property right. This is relevant to digital assets and intangible things in general, because even if they cannot be the objects of property rights and as result cannot enjoy proprietary protection, it may be possible to use possessory protections instead.

From a legal theory point of view, the concept of possession is either built on a subjective or objective doctrine with different emphases on the element of animus and corpus.[365] Ultimately, what is important here is that corpus is seen by legal theory as "*physical control*."[366] Moreover, the physical element is required under both civil and common law.[367] This element is exactly what might represent an obstacle to applying possession to digital assets, as they cannot be physically controlled in the same manner as tangible things.

The Czech Civil Code does not define possession. However, it is seen as a factual power over a thing under the Czech Civil Code as opposed to a legal one.[368] This means that possession is not a property right[369] and theoretically can be applied to intangible things.[370] The concept of possession was inspired by Austrian law[371] and it does not depart from the theoretical view described above.

Czech law also requires physical control. One past Czech Supreme Court decision is a perfect example of the difficulty in overcoming the physicality of *corpus possessionis*. In the said decision, the Supreme Court dealt with a case of an immovable not being used by its owner, but which was still being used by the detentor.[372] The court made two observation in this case — 1) factual control does not mean just physical control of a thing and 2) actual control of a thing is also possible through detention; however, the detentor must execute the physical control over the immovable.[373] The result was an ongoing requirement for the physical aspect, with the exception that it may be realized through another person. This is similar to what UNIDROIT specifically states. In their Principles, it is explicitly noted that a person cannot control digital assets through another person, as in the case of possession in certain civil law jurisdictions.[374]

---

364 EMERICH, Yaell. Possession. In: GRAZIADEI, Michele and SMITH, Lionel (eds.) *Comparative Property Law.* United Kingdom: Edward Elgar Publishing, 2017. ISBN 9781848447578, p. 171.

365 Ibid., p. 172.

366 Ibid., p. 174.

367 Ibid., p. 175.

368 ZVÁRA, Michael. § 979 In: ŠVESTKA, Jiří, DVOŘÁK, Jan et al. *Občanský zákoník: Komentář, Svazek III, (§ 976–1474).* [ASPI]. Wolters Kluwer [Accessed 2023-04-25]. ASPI_ID KO89_c2012CZ. Available at: www.aspi.cz.

369 DVOŘÁK, Jan, Jiří ŠVESTKA a Michaela ZUKLÍNOVÁ. *Občanské právo hmotné*. Praha: Wolters Kluwer, 2015. ISBN 978-80-7478-935-9, p. 99.

370 TÉGL, Petr. § 496. In: MELZER, Filip, TÉGL, Petr et al. *Občanský zákoník: velký komentář*. *Svazek III, § 419–653*. 2014, p. 243.

371 Explanatory Memorandum, p. 256.

372 Judgement of Czech Supreme Court of 17 January 2002, NS 22 Cdo 728/2000.

373 Ibid.

374 UNIDROIT. Digital Assets and Private Law. [online] April 2023 [Accessed 2023-07-20]. Available at: https://www.unidroit.org/wp-content/uploads/2023/04/C.D.-102-6-Principles-on-Digital-Assets-and-Private-Law.pdf, p. 2.

Additionally, under Czech law, possession is constructed as possession over a right, not a thing. Thus, one possesses a right (typically an ownership right) that is attached to a thing.[375] This means that possession is required where seeking to own a thing. Applied to ownership, this only applies to the possession of ownership of those intangible things that are incorporeal objects and not rights.[376]

The above carries legal consequences. Without possession, acquisitive prescription is not possible.[377] This means that in order to gain ownership, as discussed in the previous chapter, one would have to be in possession of the digital asset in the first place.

Based on the above, a question arises as to whether the newly developing concept of control can be used to interpret the current concept of possession. Through this, we could consider control to be an inherent part of possession and as a result, grant possessory rights over digital assets. The primary issue is, however, that control within the meaning of possession traditionally requires a physical element. Nevertheless, by interpreting the existing institute with digital assets in mind, we can devise a more flexible approach than the introduction of a completely new stand-alone institute concept of control.

In conclusion, a developing discourse can currently be evidenced that the concept of control might function as an equivalent to the concept of possession for digital assets. Based on the above, control still carries features that represent characteristic of possession, albeit without the need for physicality. This may overcome the barriers of current civil law, which was built for the real world. With broad interpretation, one may argue that control is just possession applied to intangible things and is an inherent part of possession. In any case, if the discussion about control and possession continues, we should prepare to answer the question of whether control should be a new property right, a new factual concept within possession, or whether it is already an inherent part of possession.

4.5 Digital Assets as Property

Previous subchapters discussed whether digital assets could be a thing and thus, whether property rights might apply. However, another important civil law category is found that may relate to digital assets, namely property. Specifically, three similar concepts exist under Czech civil law — ownership (meaning an object of ownership rights), property and assets. In the following paragraphs, I will discuss whether digital assets fall under these categories.

---

[375] § 988 Czech Civil Code.

[376] ZVÁRA, Michael. § 979 In: ŠVESTKA, Jiří, DVOŘÁK, Jan et al. *Občanský zákoník: Komentář, Svazek III, (§ 976–1474).* [ASPI]. Wolters Kluwer [Accessed 2023-04-25]. ASPI_ID KO89_c2012CZ. Available at: www.aspi.cz.

[377] Ibid.

Before delving into an analysis of digital assets, the theoretical background should be discussed. Under the Czech Civil Code, the notions of property, assets and ownership suffer from major terminological inconsistencies. As a result, all three notions can overlap and mean more or less the same.[378] Moreover, the terminology used within the Civil Code is also often misleading and inconsistent.[379]

Section 495 of the Civil Code defines both property and assets, whereby property is the "*totality of what belongs to a person.*" Assets are then defined as a broader category that includes one's property and debts. The Explanatory Memorandum describes property to be a broad category of "*things, rights and other property values that belongs to a person.*"[380] Assets are then seen as a bundle of positive and negative property values.[381]

The Czech Civil Code also includes a definition of person's ownership (within the meaning of the object of ownership right). Ownership is described as "*everything that belongs to someone, all his corporeal and incorporeal things.*"[382] Accordingly, it appears that even though the application of property rights may not be possible, the classification of a thing may actually lead to digital assets being part of one's property/assets.

The important question thus is, does the category of ownership overlap with property and assets? And, if so, then how? Commentators often describe property as tangible and intangible things, including rights.[383] This then leads to the assumption that property is the same category as ownership. However, I would argue that these three categories are actually not the same. It was the evident intention of legislators to actually make the category of property somewhat broader than the object of ownership rights, as described in the Explanatory Memorandum. It makes sense that the object of ownership is defined through tangible and intangible things, since only things can be an object of property rights. However, this does not apply to the category of property or assets. Thus, these two categories may clearly consume rights and other property values. Although this then leads to the question of why something to which one does not have ownership rights is deemed the same as a person's property. However, that is simply the way the law appears to be constructed. Consequently, the category of property (or assets) may have more overreaching functions than just serving as one's object of ownership.

---

378 DVOŘÁK, Jan, Jiří ŠVESTKA et al. *Občanské právo hmotné 3*. Praha: Wolters Kluwer, 2015. ISBN 978-80-7478-935-9, p. 27.

379 Ibid.

380 Explanatory Memorandum. [online] [Accessed 2023-11-01]. Available at: http://obcanskyzakonik.justice.cz/images/pdf/Duvodova-zprava-NOZ-konsolidovana-verze.pdf, p. 123.

381 Ibid.

382 Section 1011, Czech Civil Code.

383 KOUKAL, Pavel. § 495 [Majetek a jmění]. In: LAVICKÝ, Petr et al. *Občanský zákoník I. Obecná část (§ 1–654).* 2nd edition. Prague: C. H. Beck, 2022, p. 1525, marg. no. 2; HUBKOVÁ, Pavlína. § 495 [Majetek a jmění]. In: PETROV, Jan, VÝTISK, Michal, BERAN, Vladimír et al. *Občanský zákoník.* 2nd edition. Prague: C. H. Beck, 2023, marg. no. 1 or TÉGL, Petr. § 495. In: MELZER, Filip, TÉGL, Petr et al. *Občanský zákoník: velký komentář*. Svazek III, § 419–653. 2014, p. 235.

Another issue is whether the category of property is still limiting to some digital assets. Wide agreement exists that objects that do not have any economic value and are purely personal cannot constitute property.[384] Examples include copyrighted works or personal assets.[385] An emphasis is also made that objects or rights that have clear monetary value can be a part of one's property, which excludes all personal rights.[386] Which could exclude some digital assets from being property. This would be the case for those digital assets that are copyrighted works or have strong personal elements such as personal social media accounts. However, this appears somewhat illogical given that within the category of a thing, the discourse is much more inclusive. Evidently, in the current discourse, the line lies with stating that anything is a thing, but nothing more. Yet, it is clear that legislators enabled the Civil Code to accept such a possibility.

Understanding the concept of property is also confusing in other ways. For example, we can encounter opinions such as that ownership rights belong to one's property.[387] Does that also mean that an ownership right is a thing and thus an ownership right represents one's ownership? Some say no because that would defy logic.[388] I believe this underscores how present terminology is overly complicated and redundant, and only serves to fragment issues into unnecessary sub-issues. Furthermore, the category of property carries one meaning within civil law and another under constitutional law, which understands property to be a much wider concept that might include intellectual property.[389]

Evidently, legislators' intentions fell a little flat. As a result, the application of current laws is greatly dependable on interpretation, which may take several routes. Moreover, as demonstrated, sometimes the intended application can lead to illogical conclusions. However, since an interpretation in favour of digital assets (or at least great majority of them) is possible, a way exists to include them in property or assets.

The remaining question concerns the legal consequences of concluding that digital assets belong to property/ownership. For one, I believe that this categorization is most important for inheritance. Similarly, although one cannot control digital assets, they are still a value that could contribute to one's assets (in the economic sense).

---

[384] KOUKAL, Pavel. § 495 [Majetek a jmění]. In: LAVICKÝ, Petr et al. *Občanský zákoník I.* Obecná část (§ 1–654). 2nd edition. Prague: C. H. Beck, 2022, p. 1525, marg. no. 2 or HUBKOVÁ, Pavlína. § 495 [Majetek a jmění]. In: PETROV, Jan, VÝTISK, Michal, BERAN, Vladimír et al. *Občanský zákoník*. 2nd edition. Prague: C. H. Beck, 2023, marg. no. 1.

[385] Ibid.

[386] SVOBODA, Karel. § 495. In: ŠVESTKA, Jiří, DVOŘÁK, Jan et al. *Občanský zákoník: Komentář, Svazek I, (§ 1–654)*. [Systém ASPI]. Wolters Kluwer [Accessed 2023-12-1]. ASPI_ID KO89_a2012CZ.

[387] Ibid.

[388] TÉGL, Petr. § 496. In: MELZER, Filip, TÉGL, Petr et al. *Občanský zákoník: velký komentář. Svazek III, § 419–653.* 2014, p. 242.

[389] KOUKAL, Pavel. § 495 [Majetek a jmění]. In: LAVICKÝ, Petr et al. *Občanský zákoník I. Obecná část (§ 1–654).* 2nd edition. Prague: C. H. Beck, 2022, p. 1525, marg. no. 4.

Therefore, even if a person cannot claim property rights, it might be possible (and easier) to just claim they belong to one's property.

4.6 Digital Assets as Inheritance (Decedent's Estate)

According to Section 1475 of the Czech Civil Code, a decedent's estate consists of the decedent's entire assets and liabilities with the exception of any rights and duties exclusively tied to the decedent's personality (such as compensation for bodily harm[390]). Accordingly, the category of a decedent's estate overlaps with the category of assets. If something is considered assets, it is at the same time considered as inheritance (unless such a right or duty is purely personal). This opens up the possibility of inheriting digital assets (if, of course, the terms of service allow for it). Moreover, Czech notaries have spoken out in favour of digital inheritance in recent years, acknowledging that digital assets could be part of the decedent's estate unless contractually excluded.[391] For example, there has been a case when someone inherits a domain name (and with it the whole website).[392]

Furthermore, discussions have highlighted the importance of ensuring that passwords to accounts are left with the heirs of digital assets. Otherwise, inheritance procedures could be drawn out, given that each service provider may have different terms and conditions and access to these assets is almost impossible to achieve if the service provider does not cooperate.[393]

Additionally, it may be difficult to determine whether a decedent was the owner of certain digital assets. One such example concerns cryptoassets, as no centralized authority exists to confirm ownership.[394] Accordingly, in practice, notaries require heirs to confirm this fact. As with many other digital assets, access information is necessary for heirs to gain control over cryptoassets.[395]

The potential for digital assets to be inherited is not limited to the context of cryptoassets; it also applies to social media accounts, as discussed in Chapter 2. For

[390] FIALA, Roman. § 1475 [Dědické právo, dědictví a pozůstalost]. In: FIALA, Roman, DRÁPAL, Ljubomír et al. *Občanský zákoník IV. Dědické právo (§ 1475–1720).* 2nd edition. Prague: C. H. Beck, 2022, p. 4, marg. no. 13.

[391] KOLÁŘOVÁ, Kateřina. Digitální dědictví zatím neřešíme. Lidovky.cz. [online] 28. 11. 2018 [Accessed 2023-10-26]. Available at: https://www.lidovky.cz/byznys/digitalni-dedictvi-zatim-neresime-rika-sef-notarske-komory-neubauer.A181123_142435_ln_byznys_pravo_ssu.

[392] JANOUŠ, Vilém. Digitální dědictví: Uspořádejte svůj odkaz, ať nadobro nezmizí, radí odborníci. *Denik.cz. [*online] 19. 8. 2022 [Accessed 2023-10-26]. Available at: https://www.denik.cz/z_domova/digitalni-dedictvi-20220817.html

[393] BUŘÍNSKÁ. Barbora. Digitální dědictví řeší málokdo, přitom může ukrývat miliony. *Novinky.cz.* [online] 1. 11. 2022 [Accessed 2023-10-26]. Available at: https://www.novinky.cz/clanek/finance-digitalni-dedictvi-resi-malokdo-pritom-muze-ukryvat-miliony-40412525.

[394] KITTEL, David. Dědění Bitcoinu. *Ad Notam*. 2021, no. 2, p. 26.

[395] Ibid.

example, in 2018 the German Federal Court of Justice ruled that parents can inherit the obligations stemming from a contract between a user and the given platform, based on the principle of universal succession under the German civil code.[396] The court concluded that a social media account was digital content and that no reason could be found why digital content should be treated differently, especially since personal objects such as letters pass on to heirs according to German law.[397] The decision shows that when a clear interest by one party exists, a way can be found to interpret the law so that the social media account actually passes to the designated heirs.

However, if the principle of universal succession allows for heirs to enter into all the rights and obligations of the decedent, this should not be incidental and only occur in relation to some contracts. But practically, at present the decedent may be a party to dozens of contracts to numerous online services. And all of these would fall under the category of digital assets. Is it, therefore, really possible that heirs would become a party to every single service provided to the decedent including their email, cloud storage, social media accounts or video-on-demand services?

The advice provided by notaries points out one very important paradox — even though it may theoretically be possible to inherit digital assets, the factual state does not allow for such a transfer.

To conclude, Czech inheritance law allows for digital assets to be part of a decedent's estate so long as digital assets fall under the scope of assets (which they often will, as examined above). Nevertheless, heirs may encounter factual obstacles to the actual acquisition of the inherited digital assets. This is not different from the issues already raised by other authors from different jurisdictions, as discussed in Chapter 2. This also implies that the same obstacles that apply to assets also apply to inheritance, specifically determining what part of the decedent's estate is comprised of digital assets — i.e. whether it is the rights stemming from contracts with service providers, or an actual digital asset.

4.7 The Limits of Czech Property Law

This chapter focuses on Czech private law and discusses whether digital assets could fall under the traditional property law framework or whether they can belong to one's property, assets or inheritance. Based on the analysis, the general findings are that the limits are mostly a question of interpretation and that current laws are inadequate.

The greatest identified limit is an inflexible and obsolete system of property rights that fails to account for anything intangible or digital. The system lists many

[396] Judgement of German Federal Court of Justice from 12 July 2018, AZ III ZR 183/17.

[397] Ibid., paragraphs 56 and 57.

specific cases that apply to the physical world and quite often to the land. However, none of this can apply to the digital world.

Limitations also apply on how possession might be applied, since this is traditionally linked to physical control. As discussed, the application of possession is possible if we accept that control is an inherent part of possession and accept that the category was created for the physical world. However, this requires innovative thinking.

To conclude, even though the Czech Civil Code created an innovative concept of intangible things, it still fell short in addressing the role intangible things play in the complex system of property rights. The definition of a thing still excludes some digital assets from this classification. Moreover, trying to understand the system of property rights only leads deeper into an overly complicated rabbit hole. Indeed, what would most help the current Czech civil law property system (whether or not it concerns digital assets) is simplification and much clearer terminology.

4.8 Case Studies — Digital Assets as Things According to the Czech Law

The findings of previous chapters demonstrate that, in theory, several limitations exist to applying the property rights framework to digital assets. Many of these limitations stem from unclear interpretation or the inability to determine how the ownership of digital assets would be acquired. However, the primary question that must be answered is whether a digital asset is a thing, as it is the one category that may lead to legal consequences in terms of whether other rights may be applied. In the following sections, I will apply the definition of a thing to three selected digital assets. This text also briefly covers the relevance of determining whether digital assets are considered property or may be subject to inheritance laws or custodial agreements in certain instances and the practical obstacles that arise when applying property rights thereto. However, the primary objective of this analysis is to determine whether the three respective digital assets may be a thing under Czech law.

4.8.1 Bitcoin A revised Czech version of this subchapter was published in SOUKUPOVÁ, J. Právní povaha bitcoinu v kontextu žaloby na vydání věci. Soukromé právo. 2024

Cryptoassets, in general, represent a category of digital assets that does not fall under the intellectual property framework, as cryptoassets are not objects created by an author as an outcome of a creative process. Moreover, unlike other digital assets, there is no co-existing right (such as a contract) that would be covered as an intangible thing.[398] Accordingly, multiple recent court cases have examined the question of whether cryptoassets are subject to property rights. For example, the High Court in England concluded that a bitcoin was property in order to grant a proprietary injunction.[399] Another High Court ruling concluded that an NFT is also property for the same purposes.[400] Conversely, the Tokyo District Court, when deciding on whether a bitcoin was an object of ownership, came to the exact opposite conclusion.[401] This shows that the results of the same question can vary from one jurisdiction to another, because each jurisdiction has different conditions for recognizing something as either a thing, property or an object of ownership. At the same time, it demonstrates that with cryptoassets, a complex situation can arise where a person needs to recover their assets (i.e. to reivindicate them).

Cryptoassets exist thanks to blockchain technology, which also enables their transfer.[402] At a general level, we can divide cryptoassets into fungible and non-fungible.[403] A typical example of a non-fungible cryptoasset is a Bored Ape Yacht Club collectible, while an example of a fungible cryptoasset is exchangeable assets, or coins, such as bitcoin.[404] Sometimes, a cryptoasset is seen as a composite of a token and the linked assets or rights that exist in connection therewith.[405] However, given the existing variety of both technologies and tokens, no single definition exists for cryptoassets that would capture their technical side.[406] Moreover, a difference often exists between a coin and a token, whereby a coin is a native layer of the distributed ledger while tokens are built on an already existing layer. Similarly, factual control over cryptoassets is usually possible through a private key obtained by the holder.[407] The private key is typically the most valuable aspect of cryptoassets, as it allows for

398 ALLEN, Jason G.; Rauchs, Michel; BLANDIN, Apolline; BEAR, Keith. Legal and Regulatory Considerations for Digital Assets. [online] [Accessed 2023-05-23]. Available at: https://www.jbs.cam.ac.uk/wp-content/uploads/2020/10/2020-ccaf-legal-regulatory-considerations-report.pdf, p. 13.

399 Judgement of High Court of England from 2019, *AA v Persons Unknown*, EWHC 3556, English High Court.

400 Judgement of High Court of England from 2023 *Lavinia Deborah Osbourne v Persons Unknown Category A & Ors* [2023] EWHC 39.

401 Judgement of Tokyo District Court from 2015 *Z1 v Mt. Gox,* reference number 25541521.

402 CHAN, Timothy. The nature of property in cryptoassets. Online. *Legal studies (Society of Legal Scholars)*. 2023, vol. 43, no. 3, p. 482.

403 WYCZIK, Jakub. The Property Law of Crypto Tokens [online] November 2023 [Accessed 2024-02-01] Available at: SSRN: https://ssrn.com/abstract=4620033 or http://dx.doi.org/10.2139/ssrn.4620033, p. 9.

404 Ibid.

405 UK LAW COMMISSION. Digital Assets Consultation Paper. [online] 28. 7. 2022 [Accessed 2024-05-20]. Available at: https://cloud-platform-e218f50a4812967ba1215eaecede923f.s3.amazonaws.com/uploads/sites/30/2022/07/Digital-Assets-Consultation-Paper-Law-Commission-1.pdf, p. 156.

406 UK Jurisdiction Taskforce. Legal statement on the cryptoasstes and smart contracts. [online] November 2019 [Accessed 2024-02-01] Available at: https://www.blockchain4europe.eu/wp-content/uploads/2021/05/6.6056_JO_Cryptocurrencies_Statement_FINAL_WEB_111119-1.pdf, p. 9–10.

407 Ibid., p. 10.

control. As the title of this subchapter indicates, I will now focus solely on bitcoin and consider whether it can be a thing under Czech law.

Bitcoin is probably the most widely known cryptocurrency. It is built on a distributed ledger (blockchain) and users can buy or sell the bitcoins directly without a third entity, while each transaction remains publicly accessible in the distributed ledger.[408] What makes bitcoins different from other cryptocurrencies is that is runs on its own native ledger. Which means technically no token is present.[409] Some commentators interpret bitcoin to be a mere entry about a transaction in a database.[410] Another factor that distinguishes bitcoin from other cryptocurrencies is its mining process. While bitcoin functions on a "proof-of-work" model, ethereum blockchain uses a "proof-of-stake" mechanism.[411] Finally, the method used for the record of transactions differs among cryptocurrencies. For bitcoin, an "unspent transaction output" model is used (as opposed to, e.g., Ethereum which uses an "account balance" model).[412] In practice this means that ether transfers do not involve any traceable tokens and only transfer value from one account to another. Conversely, when bitcoin is transferred, no individual bitcoins are tracked.[413]

Mining is not the only possibility for obtaining bitcoins. Currently, it is far more common for customers to purchase bitcoins through a cryptocurrency exchange such as Coinbase or Binance.[414] As customers conduct transactions, these are subject to the terms of service of each exchange. Coinbase, for instance, holds the purchased cryptoassets for the customer on a custodial basis and the customer is deemed the owner of these assets.[415] Customers also require a crypto wallet to store purchased cryptocurrencies, which is often again provided by an exchange in the cloud, and which stores all the encryption necessary.[416] In any case, the factual ability to control bitcoin is often linked to access to a private key. Without a private key, the user loses their ability to make any transactions.[417]

For a bitcoin to be a thing, it must fulfil the criteria of being different from a person and to serve the needs of people. I believe both criteria are fulfilled, since bitcoins are not connected to persons in any way, contrary to, for example, copyrighted

408 ASHFORD, Kate and ADAMS, Michael. What Is Bitcoin and How Does It Work? *Forbes*. [online] 8 June 2022 [Accessed 2024-02-16] Available at: https://www.forbes.com/advisor/investing/cryptocurrency/what-is-bitcoin/.

409 What is a Token? [online] [Accessed 2024-02-16] Available at: https://www.coinbase.com/learn/crypto-basics/what-is-a-token.

410 KITTEL, David. Dědění Bitcoinu. *Ad Notam*. 2021, no. 2, p. 26.

411 CHAN, Timothy. The Nature of Property in Cryptoassets. Online. *Legal studies (Society of Legal Scholars)*. 2023, vol. 43, no. 3, p. 483.

412 Ibid.

413 Ibid.

414 Ibid.

415 Coinbase Terms of service, paragraph 5.19. [online] [Accessed 2024-02-16] Available at: https://www.coinbase.com/legal/user_agreement/ireland_europe.

416 Ibid.

417 CHAN, Timothy. The nature of property in cryptoassets. Online. *Legal studies (Society of Legal Scholars)*. 2023, vol. 43, no. 3, p. 497.

works. Moreover, given its monetary value, it serves the needs of people. The need is often connected to whether the object is controllable.[418] However, given the possibility of factually controlling bitcoins though a wallet and to conduct trade and transfers, I find this criterion to be fulfilled. Czech law also does not see its intangible nature as an obstacle.

What might be an issue for bitcoins to be a thing is the implicit requirement to be capable of being an object of ownership rights. However, given the vast possibility of factually controlling bitcoins, it appears that despite their intangible nature, they might be an object of ownership rights. A stricter interpretation may limit application only to tangible things, rendering the category of intangible objects meaningless. Furthermore, bitcoins have been recognized as both property and part of a decedent's estate in legal literature.[419] The only limitation here is factual, namely that one needs a private key to gain access to control bitcoins, and in the case of inheritance, to actually inherit it.[420]

Bitcoin has also been recognized as an intangible, movable, fungible thing by multiple authors.[421] Which means an evident larger consensus on its legal categorization under Czech property law. It must be emphasized, however, that although a consensus exists that bitcoin is a thing and property under Czech law, no analysis has been carried out into the exact nature of the "thing" in question — be it a token, coin, underlying data or something else. For example, some argue that the "thing" is the transactional ability that allows for a valid blockchain transfer.[422] Here, I would suggest a pragmatic approach. Digital assets and especially crypto assets are exploited for their economic value.[423] The value is not solely connected to one aspect of the bitcoin (or other crypt assets) but to the complete bundle of interconnected elements — be it the underlying data, transactional ability, private key, token and so on. The specific characteristics will always differ based on the concrete cryptoassets. Moreover, it is apparent that any more detailed analysis only leads to a conclusion under which some cryptoassets can be subject to property while others cannot.[424] In any case, the complexity of determining the exact object of property rights demonstrates just how the application differs to tangible and intangible things.

[418] HUBKOVÁ, Pavlína. § 489 [Pojem věci v právním smyslu]. In: PETROV, Jan, VÝTISK, Michal, BERAN, Vladimír et al. Občanský zákoník. 2nd edition. Prague: C. H. Beck, 2023, marg. no. 7.

[419] See e.g. VANKÁTOVÁ, Iveta. Digitální dědictví – aneb jak se dědí bitcoin. *Ad Notam*, 2023, vol. 4, pp. 25–30.

[420] Ibid.

[421] For instance, KITTEL, David. Dědění Bitcoinu. *Ad Notam*. 2021, no. 2; JAREŠ, Adam. Kryptoměny a občanské právo. *Revue pro právo a technologie*, vol 11. no. 21; KUNDRÁTOVÁ, Petra and EISENREICH, Jan. Právní aspekty kryptoměn. AUC Iuridica. 2018. vol. LXIV, no. 1; VANKÁTOVÁ, Iveta. Digitální dědictví – aneb jak se dědí bitcoin. *Ad Notam*, 2023, vol. 4, pp. 25–30.

[422] CHAN, Timothy. The Nature of Property in Cryptoassets. Online. *Legal studies (Society of Legal Scholars)*. 2023, vol. 43, no. 3.

[423] Ibid., p. 495.

[424] Ibid., p. 489.

Recently, a Czech district court dealt with a *rei vindicatio* claim for bitcoin in which it was also recognized that bitcoin was a thing under Czech law.[425] In this case, the plaintiff demanded 3,06 bitcoin from the defendant with whom he had previously entered into a custodial agreement. Since the defendant failed to perform its obligations under the agreement, the plaintiff sought to recover the bitcoins. In its ruling, the court concluded that a bitcoin is a fungible thing according to Section 499 of the Czech Civil Code.[426] Unfortunately, the court did not explain how it reached this conclusion. The court only noted that since bitcoin is a fungible, generic thing, it can be recovered and it is not necessary to claim its monetary value.[427] This is notable, since, in general, it should not be possible to recover intangible generic things.[428] Moreover, the court did not consider whether the given bitcoin belonged to the plaintiff in the sense that it was his ownership to which he had a *rei vindicatio* claim, or whether the plaintiff could distinguish his bitcoins from others. Furthermore, the court did not consider the nature of the contract, which was a custodial agreement. This means that the court implicitly acknowledged that the plaintiff was in the position of a beneficiary and the owner, and that the bitcoin was the plaintiff's property.

As noted in the previous chapter, the Czech Civil Code requires the owner, when filing a rei vindication claim, to distinguish the thing from other things of the same kind, or, in case of things that are mixed with others (such as money), to provide circumstances which allow a determination of ownership.[429] Accordingly, the district court decision does not provide any definitive legal opinion, as it did not delve into the important questions surrounding property rights to bitcoin. This is a similar result as in common law cases heard by the English High Court where it recognized bitcoin[430] and NFT[431] as property for the purpose of property injunction but did not provide any subsequent argumentation as how the ownership was acquired.

In conclusion, bitcoin appears to be a digital asset that can be classified as a thing under Czech law without any obstacles. However, given its technical and intangible nature, obstacles may exist to either effectively transferring it (e.g. upon death) or to applying other property law institutes (such as a *rei vindicatio* claims). On the other hand, it appears that the application of a property law framework found its way into court practice, thus any future reluctance to apply it would require a careful explanation by the court.

---

425 Judgement of the District Court Prague-west from 5 December 2022, 16 C 359/2020-187.

426 Ibid, paragraph 20.

427 Ibid.

428 Comp. DOBROVOLNÁ, Eva. § 1040 [Reivindikační žaloba]. In: PETROV, Jan, VÝTISK, Michal, BERAN, Vladimír et al. *Občanský zákoník*. 2nd edition. Prague: C. H. Beck, 2023, marg. no. 3.

429 Section 1041 of Czech Civil Code.

430 Judgement of High Court of England from 2019, *AA v Persons Unknown*, EWHC 3556 English High Court.

431 Judgement of English High Court 2023, *Lavinia Deborah Osbourne v Persons Unknown* Category A & Ors, EWHC 39.

4.8.2 Social Media Account

The topic of property rights to social media accounts often arises upon death and when they may be subject to inheritance, as was discussed in Chapter 2. As observed, social media accounts are primarily governed by the terms and conditions of each platform in which the service providers often restrict any rights over the accounts and as a result, social media accounts are excluded from being subject to inheritance. For example, Meta's Terms of Service for Facebook and Instagram specifically state that a user cannot share their password or in any manner transfer their account without the company's consent; or, in Instagram's case, sell or attempt to sell the account.[432] Similarly, Linkedin's User Agreement does not allow for any transfer of the account and access by other parties is only authorised in cases when the account was purchased for someone else to use.[433] Moreover, even in individual states within the US which have adopted RUFADAA, the terms of service will still prevail in cases when the deceased did not leave any information about access.[434]

Social media accounts have a complex technical structure, and they often allow for storing a user's personal information, files, photographs or videos. This can make the case of them being an object of property rights complicated, as one must first determine the exact object — i.e., the URL address, the social media page, the access information or something else. Furthermore, given their multifunctionality, it is possible to argue that such accounts are nothing more than a service provided to the user. This is, for example, how X (formerly Twitter) sees its platform in their terms of service. There, the company specifically stipulates that they are only giving users a license to use their services and that these services are protected by copyright, trademark and similar laws.[435] Therefore, the service provided to the user is unambiguously affected by the intellectual property interests of the service providers which exist in their structure by default.

From a user perspective, social media accounts may be extremely valuable, especially if an account has a high number of followers. In such cases, the account may be subject to monetization. On top of that, social media accounts often work to store messages, photographs or files. Thus, many reasons exist why it would be reasonable to treat social media accounts as an object of property rights. For example, if a user has a valuable account, it will allow them to sell it or to use it as a security.

---

[432] Article 3.1. of Terms of service. [online] [Accessed 2024-02-20]. Available at: https://www.facebook.com/legal/terms?paipv=0&eav=AfbEG1C7kb1GGQnl7-VCmby6Q_A1fsdtcC78BLMifuY-Hudl5uv0CWzKNYtGfvmfaHs&_rdr; Instagram's Terms of Use. How you can't use Instagram. [online] [Accessed 2024-02-20]. Available at: https://help.instagram.com/581066165581870?cms_id=581066165581870.

[433] Linkedin's User Agreement. 2.2 Your Account. [online] [Accessed 2024-02-20]. Available at: https://www.linkedin.com/legal/user-agreement.

[434] Section 5 RUFADAA.

[435] X's Terms of Service. Your License to Use the Service. [online] [Accessed 2024-02-20]. Available at: https://twitter.com/en/tos.

Similarly, one could authorise a third party to manage an account under a custodial agreement. In some cases, if someone gives third-party access and they do not return it, one may need to use a *rei vindicatio* claim to gain the access back. All of these scenarios occur in the real world (which thus often breaches the terms and conditions of the respective service provider). Reasonable grounds exist, therefore, why users would want their social media accounts to be their property.

Moreover, with social media accounts, it is arguably the right to access them (as a service) which matters to users the most. Therefore, the arguments here may go strongly in the direction of looking at them as intangible things in the form of rights. However, such rights are relative in nature and do not allow for permanent or repeated exercise, rendering them ineligible for inclusion under Sections 496 or 979 of the Czech Civil Code.[436]

On the other hand, social media accounts are similar to domain names. It could also be argued that access information (logins and passwords) could be separated and treated as things. After all, similarly to domain names, ownership of access information is what allows users to create their own social media pages in a similar fashion to how ownership of a domain allows for the creation of a website.

As is apparent from the above consideration, the argumentation for social media accounts to either be or not be a thing can branch in many directions. The primary question is, however, whether they are a thing according to Czech property law. Only after answering this question is it possible to consider the resulting legal consequences, such as which property rights apply or whether it is possible to inherit such accounts.

Applying the requirements for something to be a thing under Czech law, we can reach the conclusion that none of the criteria are likely fulfilled. Firstly, although social media accounts have an economic or social value to their users (and thus might serve their needs), it is unclear whether they could be considered controllable within the meaning of this requirement. Typically, uncontrollable forces of nature such as electricity have not been considered as serving the needs of people.[437] Moreover, if one factually cannot control something, even in the legal sense, it does not fulfil the applicable requirements.[438] Social media accounts are governed by often very strict terms and conditions, which leave no space for either their transfer or trading. Moreover, the respective conditions often even prohibit providing access to others. As a result, the user has no factual or legal control. The same would apply even if the "thing" is the rights stemming from the contract, since contractual rights are, as discussed in the previous section, not considered

[436] Judgement of the Czech Supreme Court 23 Cdo 3320/2020 from 30 August 2021, and Judgement of the Czech Supreme Court 33 Cdo 3720/2020 from 25 November 2021.

[437] HUBKOVÁ, Pavlína. § 489 [Pojem věci v právním smyslu]. In: PETROV, Jan, VÝTISK, Michal, BERAN, Vladimír et al. *Občanský zákoník*. 2nd edition. Prague: C. H. Beck, 2023, marg. no. 7.

[438] KOUKAL, Pavel. § 489 [Pojem věci v právním smyslu]. In: LAVICKÝ, Petr et al. *Občanský zákoník I. Obecná část (§ 1–654)*. 2nd edition Prague: C. H. Beck, 2022, p. 1495, marg. no. 27.

a thing because they are not capable of a "real" transfer and only an assignment of the contract is factually occurring.[439]

The above makes the criterion of being controllable and capable of serving one's needs hard to fulfil. On the other hand, social media accounts still provide users a platform which can be customized to their own liking and sometimes even be monetized. Therefore, one could argue, a certain level of control exists, because accounts can still be used in multiple ways which serve those who operate them. I would normally incline to the second option, mostly because it allows for a broad category of a thing. But here, I incline to the first option, mostly because social media accounts (similarly to in-game objects or email accounts) rely too much on a service provider's technical infrastructure and are bound by the provisions of contracts.[440]

Fulfilling the second condition, being different from a person, is similarly complicated for social media accounts. Traditionally, expressions of a personal nature such as letters are not considered things under Czech law.[441] This limitation may have significant consequences when it comes to personal social media accounts, especially since social media accounts often store personal conversations. Due to their personal nature, Szwajdler, for example, argues that social media accounts (or private email accounts) should not be inheritable, either at all or only in a limited manner.[442] Moreover, personal media accounts are often a reflection of users' personalities and a means to share every aspect of their private lives. Therefore, I would argue that because of this limitation, personal social media accounts cannot be considered things under Czech law.

The situation could be different for non-personal accounts, such as company social media accounts. Here, the personal aspect of sharing one's private life is not present, as these types of account typically have a purely business nature. The separate legal consequences for two types of the same thing might appear unfair; however, an opposite argument would go against legislators' intentions to not cover personal expressions under property rights. Moreover, business accounts might still not pass the first condition discussed above. Therefore, ultimately, no social media account can be considered a thing under Czech law.

The above conclusion has the consequence that social media accounts cannot be the object of property rights, including that they cannot be an object of ownership.

---

439 HUBKOVÁ, Pavlína. § 496 [Věci hmotné a nehmotné]. In: PETROV, Jan, VÝTISK, Michal, BERAN, Vladimír et al. *Občanský zákoník.* 2nd edition. Prague: C. H. Beck, 2023, marg. no. 7.

440 Comp. Digital Assets Consultation Paper. [online] 28. 7. 2022 [Accessed 2023-07-20]. Available at: https://s3-eu-west-2.amazonaws.com/lawcom-prod-storage-11jsxou24uy7q/uploads/2022/07/Digital-Assets-Consultation-Paper-Law-Commission-1.pdf, p. 124.

441 SVOBODA, Karel. § 489. In: ŠVESTKA, Jiří et al. *Občanský zákoník: Komentář, Svazek I, (§ 1–654).* [Systém ASPI]. Wolters Kluwer [Accessed 2023-04-25]. ASPI_ID KO89_a2012CZ. Available at: www.aspi.cz.

442 SZWAJDLER, Paweł. "Digital assets and inheritance law: How to create fundamental principles of digital succession system?" Online. *International journal of law and information technology.* 2023, vol. 31, no. 2, p. 157.

Moreover, one cannot use *rei vindicatio* claims where another person gains access to the given account. Similarly, even if the account is of value, it can hardly be used as a security or transferred to a third party.

The next question is whether social media accounts are part of a decedent's estate, despite such accounts not being classified as a thing. And if so, whether it would be in the form of the actual account or in the form of the obligation stemming from the contract with the given service provider.

I will briefly address this, because the topic of inheriting digital assets is often connected to social media accounts, as discussed in Chapter 2. Multiple documented cases have arisen when persons wanted or needed to access a deceased person's social media account. For example, parents in Germany sought to access their late daughter's social media account to determine whether she had committed suicide. The outcome of the dispute was discussed in a previous section of this book and demonstrates the possibility of inheriting not an account itself, but in line with the principle of universal succession, to enter into the deceased's rights stemming from a contract.[443] The motive of German parents seeking to gain access to their children's social media after death was not a unique case. Similarly, parents in the US state of Virginia pursued the same interest by lobbying for a new law which would allow such access to parents or guardians.[444] Accordingly, some cases are certainly found when a need exists to access a deceased person's social media accounts.

As noted in the previous section, a decedent's estate consists of the decedent's entire assets and liabilities with the exception of those rights and duties that are exclusively tied to the decedent's personality.[445] Furthermore, Czech inheritance law is built on the principle of universal succession and, as a result, heirs enter into all the rights and obligations of the deceased.[446] Moreover, the principle should guarantee that heirs will have the exactly same contractual position as was held by the deceased.[447] This opens up the possibility that although social media accounts are not a thing, they may be subject to inheritance, and heirs may inherit them and enter into contracts with service providers. As the German court observed, the service provided by the given social media platform was merely technical and the identity of the party to which it was being provided is irrelevant.[448] Thus, it is not an obligation that would from either side be exclusive to the decedent. Additionally, it was

---

443 Judgement of German Federal Court of Justice from 12 July 2018, AZ III ZR 183/17, paragraph 57.

444 NGAK, Chenda. "Couple wins right to view dead child's Facebook account." *CBS news*. [online] 20 February 2013 [Accessed 2024-02-22]. Available at: https://www.cbsnews.com/news/couple-wins-right-to-view-dead-childs-facebook-account/.

445 Section 1475 of the Czech Civil Code.

446 MUZIKÁŘ, Martin. § 1475 [Dědické právo, pozůstalost, dědic, dědictví]. In: PETROV, Jan, VÝTISK, Michal, BERAN, Vladimír et al. *Občanský zákoník*. 2nd edition. Prague: C. H. Beck, 2023, marg. no. 10.

447 MIKK, Tiina, SEIN, Karin. Digital Inheritance: Heirs's Rights to Claim Access to Online Accounts under Estonian Law. *Juridica International*. 2018, vol. 27.

448 Judgement of German Federal Court of Justice from 12 July 2018, AZ III ZR 183/17, paragraph 42 and 43.

exactly the principle of universal succession that allowed for the rights stemming from a contract to be passed onto the heirs in the German case.[449] Similarly, Italian law is in line with the principle of universal succession and allows for an account to be inherited where a contract does not exclude it.[450]

The only (practical) issue is that the respective terms and conditions would not explicitly exclude the passing of the service to a third party, and the service provider would have to provide the necessary access information. But from the point of the law, it is apparent that Czech law allows for the inheritance of an obligation, and in case of a dispute, one could potentially gain access as in the German case. The only obstacles to why a person could not inherit a social media account (or, more precisely, access to it) is simply that the service provider would not allow it. This conclusion, however, only means that either a regulatory interest exists to void the service provider's terms and conditions, or no such interest exists, and a system where service providers decide for themselves is the desired one.

The above demonstrates that reasons exist why property interests in social media accounts are a pressing issue — either because they are a source of profit, because they need third parties to manage them, because they have a value of their own, or because a need exists to gain access after death. However, the technical structure of these accounts is heavily reliant on the service provider's infrastructure and often includes elements that are subject to the service provider's intellectual property rights. Therefore, recognizing social media accounts as things is not possible unless the interpretation is stretched far enough so it passes both applicable conditions. However, social media accounts function more as a service and are closely tied to personal data and personal rights. Thus, it is unlikely that the current property law framework can be applied directly to them. This does not rule out the possibility that a contract itself might not be inheritable. As demonstrated, the law, in line with the principle of universal succession, allows for heirs to enter into contracts with the respective service providers. The only restrictions here are practical, since the given terms and conditions often do not allow for any transfer to third parties. This opens up a question of whether legislative changes should occur to enable property rights application, or whether the rights of a user to a service should be covered by a completely different set of rules than property rights.

4.8.3 AI-generated Works

The ability to create artworks using AI tools has made it possible to produce images quickly and inexpensively for various purposes. However, this has also sparked debate on how such imagery, or another audio or visual content is protected by law.

[449] Judgement of German Federal Court of Justice from 12 July 2018, AZ III ZR 183/17, paragraph 70.

[450] PATTI, Francesco Paolo, BARTOLINI, Francesca. Digital inheritance and post mortem data protection: The Italian reform. Bocconi Legal Studies Research Paper Series. June 2019, no. 339974, p. 4.

At present, a consensus evidently exists that AI artworks are not protected by copyright due to the lack of originality and creativity, which has also been supported by few court decisions.[451] This means that at least from the intellectual property point of view, anyone can use and spread the AI-generated content. Therefore, the important question with AI-generated artworks is whether they can be owned.[452] Since copyright is not a means of protection for a vast number of AI-generated works, a possibility exists to claim traditional ownership over these works.

As with some other digital assets, the possibility of generating an individual's own AI imagery is provided as a service. And this service is yet again governed by its provider's terms of use. Similarly to social media accounts, the factual control over AI-generated works is governed by the terms and conditions of the respective AI tool provider. These contracts typically limit what the user may do once their artwork is created. However, service providers often grant users far more rights than in the case of social media accounts. For example, Midjourney stipulates in its Terms of Service that the user owns the created artwork unless they are a company with more than $1,000,000 USD yearly revenue.[453] At the same time, the user grants Midjourney a license to any generated artworks[454]. Similarly, OpenAI also grants its users full ownership of their artwork generated by DALL-E.[455] Therefore, while service providers still construct their terms as service provisions, they do not claim any ownership over the respective artwork. This probably reflects the outcome of a recent US court decision, which concluded that AI-generated artworks are not protected by copyright.[456] But it might also be the result of a factual state in which, compared to social media accounts, service providers do not have any factual control over AI-generated artworks because they can be simply copied.

The marketability of the artworks in question is debatable. AI art is broadly and freely available for anyone to create with a simple prompt. It is therefore presently unclear if anyone would be interested in purchasing or protecting such AI-generated art. Compared to other digital assets, AI-generated works do not pose such economic or social value. And value is usually the reason why people opt out for the property law to protect their digital assets. On the other hand, there may be instances

---

[451] E.g. Judgement of the Municipal Court in Prague from 11 October 2023, 10 C 13/2023-16, or the Judgement of the United States District Court for the District of Columbia from 18 August 2023, Civil Action no. 22-1564 (BAH).

[452] LEMLEY, Mark A. How Generative AI Turns Copyright Upside Down. [online] June 2023. [Accessed 2024-28-02]. Available from: https://papers.ssrn.com/sol3/papers.cfm?abstract_id=4517702, p. 3.

[453] Section 4. Content Rights of Midjourney's Terms of Service [online]. [Accessed 2024-02-26]. Available at: https://docs.midjourney.com/docs/terms-of-service.

[454] Section 4. Rights you Give to Midjourney. of Midjourney's Terms of Service [online]. [Accessed 2024-02-26]. Available from: https://docs.midjourney.com/docs/terms-of-service.

[455] Terms of Use of OpenAI. Content. [online]. [Accessed 2024-02-26]. Available at: https://openai.com/policies/terms-of-use.

[456] Judgement of the United States District Court for the District of Columbia from 18 August 2023, Civil Action no. 22-1564 (BAH).

in which someone might decide to protect their AI generated work. AI is starting to be used more and more for purposes of creating various business materials, either visual or textual. Such materials are probably already being protected under various confidentiality agreements. But it may be a question of time until companies will try to enforce property regimes in case someone will use their AI generated contents. Such scenario is not different from cases when companies seek to protect their data by imposing property regime. The only difference here is that such was generated by a tool rather than directly created by the company.

If we want to apply traditional property law then it is necessary to firstly establish whether AI-generated artwork fulfils the definition of an intangible thing under Czech law. Since AI-generated artworks are not generally considered copyrighted works, the condition of being different from a person is fulfilled. They may also fulfil the condition to serve the needs of people, since they are typically used for promotional activities. Moreover, as demonstrated above, the respective terms and conditions give users vast control over such works — meaning users can use them any way they wish. This leads to the conclusion that the requirement of being capable of control is also fulfilled. AI-generated artworks are also not a part of a service, as they are separated in the process of creation. Which means that, unlike social media accounts, no need applies to consider whether the thing is the contract or the actual artwork. Therefore, I believe that AI-generated artworks are an intangible thing within the meaning of Czech property law.

Since AI-generated artworks fulfil the definition of a thing, the question concerns who has ownership of such artworks and how such ownership is acquired. As demonstrated above, the terms and conditions of AI tools may allow users to hold the rights to their generated artworks. However, the question is whether users could acquire ownership only by means of writing a set of prompts, which then leads to a picture being generated. I believe the answer to this will always depend on each jurisdiction and the recognized ways of obtaining ownership thereto. Some jurisdictions allow for the acquisition of ownership based on the creation of a thing.[457] Then the test would depend on whether creation via the inputting of prompts could be analogical to traditional cases of creation.

If the answer is given according to Czech law, opinions are found that such ownership may be acquired either through appropriation or by specification.[458] However, such a conclusion is slightly short-sighted. The institute of appropriation requires possession, which is by nature physical.[459] This means that in order to be applied to the digital intangible's environment, a broad interpretation of possession is required. Otherwise, I do not agree that appropriation is possible

[457] E.g. the Netherlands, as stated in the Judgement of the Netherlands Commercial Court from 21 April 2023 NCC 22/018, paragraph 4.36.

[458] MLADÁ, Klára. (Ne)díla umělé inteligence a počiny dalších (ne)autorů. *Obchodněprávní revue*, 2023, no. 2, p. 122–125.

[459] JANOUŠEK, Lubomír. § 1045 [Právo na přivlastnění si věci]. In: PETROV, Jan, VÝTISK, Michal, BERAN, Vladimír et al. *Občanský zákoník*. 2nd edition. Prague: C. H. Beck, 2023, marg. no. 2.

for intangible things such as AI generated work. Similarly, the concept of specification is tailored to situations when a new thing is created from things already belonging to previous owners. This means, again, that the data from which the AI generated artwork is derived from would have to be in someone's ownership and mostly, that they are recognized as things in the first place. Again, I do not find the institute of specification in its current form suitable for ownership acquisition of AI generated works.

Therefore, ultimately, even if users are permitted by contract to use a generated artwork however they like, they still do not own it. This means mostly that they cannot apply any ownership protection claims in the case someone else uses the artworks they have generated. On the other hand, the respective contracts may serve as proof of ownership. It is important to mention that different jurisdictions have different rules for acquiring ownership. The fact that Czech law is not suitable to derive such ownership does not mean that under different jurisdiction, the ownership would not be possible.

The above also demonstrates that practically all AI-generated works might not carry any true value. Furthermore, since no legal protections apply and the generated art itself is not unique, no practical need currently exists for any traditional property law to apply. Without value, one cannot, for example, use artworks as a security. Similarly, no need would exist to transfer rights, since no one would be interested in owning something without value.

4.8.4 Concluding Remarks

The analysis performed in the previous section demonstrated significant differences between the three selected digital assets when it comes to the application of the traditional property law framework. The observations are summarized as follows:

- The three selected digital assets function differently. This means that the users have a different margin of factual control over them.
- While social media accounts and AI-generated artworks are governed by the terms of service of the given service provider, generally no service provider exists in the case of bitcoin. This being said, a contract with a custodian may still be entered into when a customer purchases bitcoins, and such a contract may limit factual control.
- Social media accounts are designed with complete dependency on service providers while with bitcoin this dependence may be lower when customers hold a private key and wallet. With AI-generated artworks, once created, users may freely control what they do with an artwork and the service provider is only necessary as a provider for the tool that allows the artwork to be generated.
- The need for *rei vindicatio* or inheritance is much lower with AI-generated artworks, since they are not dependent on a service provider or custodian.

The below table summarizes the observed differences between all three digital assets.

	Social Media Account	**Bitcoin**	**AI-generated artwork**
governed by terms of service	YES	NO	YES
interference with data protection or privacy laws	YES	NO	NO
interference with intellectual property law	PARTIAL	NO	IN MOST CASES, NO[460]
provided as a service	YES	NO	PARTIALLY
categorized as digital content under DCD	YES	POTENTIALLY	YES
Intangible thing under Czech law	NO	YES	YES
monetary value	POSSIBLE	YES	IN MOST CASES, NO
factual control	LOW	MODERATE	HIGH
conditions to be inherited	– terms of service permission – no interference with privacy – access information available	– possession of private key – witness to confirm it belonged to the deceased	– access to the device – possible terms of service permission

It must be emphasized that the table above only captures general differences. Additional differences may exist, even within each category, depending on the specific technological infrastructure or concrete contractual provisions.

Moreover, a different level of legal certainty applies when it comes to determining if a digital asset is a thing. However, arguments can be heard supporting both interpretations — i.e. all of them being, or not being, a thing. Therefore, it will ultimately depend on individual judges to determine towards which interpretation they incline.

To conclude, the primary underlying issue with digital assets is the legal uncertainty concerning which law applies to them, as no settled interpretation or application has yet been developed.

460 This conclusion is based on the current consensus that most AI-generated works are not protected as copyrighted works, largely due to the fact that no author exists to which the rights would be attributed, or no creativity is present, However, in some cases, AI-generated works could reach an IP standard if the author's prompts fulfil the criteria for creativity.

5 WHAT SHOULD THE LEGISLATOR DO?: ADDRESSING THE LEGISLATIVE GAPS

The underlying theme of this monograph is that the legal framework for digital assets is, unlike with tangible things, uncertain. As a result, all interactions users make in the online environment are governed by contracts, which pose as a one-stop-shop instrument in this context.[461] And while these contracts provide the necessary regulation tailored to specific digital assets, intellectual property law can only be applied to some of these assets, which leaves open the question of whether traditional property law can provide users with the necessary protection of their digital assets. However, as demonstrated in Chapter 4, the scope of application of traditional property law is limited because the framework was created to be applied to the physical world and thus application mostly relies on a broad interpretation of existing institutes. Moreover, as the analysis showed, application varies with different digital assets. In this final chapter, I will summarize the identified legislative gaps under Czech law and discuss potential legislative changes that might be desirable for greater legal certainty.

5.1 Legislative Gaps Concerning Digital Assets

Chapter 4 addressed the suitability of Czech property law for application to digital assets. As the conducted analysis demonstrated, several legal gaps and deficiencies hinder proper application. These will be addressed in the following subchapters.

Disparity between Property Rights in Tangible and Intangible Objects

The primary deficit in Czech property law is a disparity between how property rights are applied to tangible and intangible things. This issue is not limited to digital assets; it can be applied to anything that falls under the category of intangible things. Nonetheless, this disparity has been criticized as unjustified in the context of digital assets and cyberspace.[462]

---

[461] MACDONALD, Michaela. *The Case for Virtual Property*. Dissertation thesis. Queen Mary University of London, 2016, p. 178.

[462] Ibid.

As demonstrated in Chapter 4, traditional property rights under Czech law do not apply to intangible things automatically. Rather, a need exists to evaluate whether their nature allows for a proper application. Moreover, no provisions concern either property or inheritance law that would directly address digital assets, so as to offer guidance from legislators to take the "correct" approach. At the same time, the Czech Civil Code contains many provisions tailored for situations in the real, material world, such as alluvium[463], or special cases of acquiring ownership in situations such as public auctions.[464] Consequently, it is not unusual that legislators created specific norms in order to clarify certain situations concerning property rights. Which is why it is logical to address digital assets as well.

A certain indicator that the Czech Civil Code inclines to the recognition of digital assets as things is incorporated in the implementation of the Digital Content Directive. As discussed in Chapter 3, the notion of digital content largely overlaps with the notion of digital assets. As a part of the transposition of the directive, the Czech Civil Code was amended so as to contain a provision stating that digital content is a thing in digital form.[465] Referring to digital content as a thing in digital form was already argued as evidence that digital content is a thing in the legal sense under Czech law.[466] However, the provision itself is not clear enough to definitively reach this conclusion. Especially since it is not clear whether legislators meant things in the legal sense or not and only used the word in order to give the addressees an idea of what is meant by digital content.

Consequently, legislators should make it clear whether intangible things (including digital assets) can be the objects of property rights. This may be achieved by, for example, allowing only tangible things to be objects or by adding further details to the category of intangible things. If it truly was the intention of lawmakers that it applies to digital assets as well, some conceptual changes to the law are needed. Specifically, Section 979 of the Czech Civil Code, which contains a provision that limits the scope of application of property rights, would benefit from a more definitive wording that would not leave commentators arguing that property rights only apply to those intangible things whose nature allows it. Alternatively, some guidance should be created on how to determine whether the nature of an intangible thing allows for its application. Until such changes are made to the law, interpretations may go in both directions.

Legal Uncertainty

The above-described issues are closely connected to another issue — legal uncertainty about the applicable legal framework. As the application of traditional

[463] Section 1068, Czech Civil Code.

[464] Section 1109, Czech Civil Code.

[465] § 2389a Czech civil code.

[466] LIMBERGOVÁ, Zuzana. Směrnice o digitálním obsahu a jejich implementace v právním řádu ČR. *Revue pro právo a technologie*. 2022, vol. 13, no. 25, p. 248.

property law to the three selected digital assets demonstrated significant technical differences exist between such assets, resulting in different outcomes in the application of the law. The issue of treating digital assets as one large group and umbrella term will be addressed in the following chapters. Here, I will only discuss why I consider the current legislative framework to be deficient in the sense that it causes legal uncertainty.

As discussed throughout this work, the legal framework applicable to digital assets is uncertain and digital assets can fall within many legal frameworks.[467] However, since digital assets can be valuable to either users or service providers, the core question concerns who has the rights in them and the nature of these rights, with traditional property law being often discussed as a legal framework that should theoretically provide subjects with the desired rights. However, Czech property law does not provide a clear legal framework to provide subjects with a definitive answer as to who owns digital assets, or whether they can even be owned in the first place. Where those digital assets are protected by an intellectual property right framework this is at least partially covered, because the respective rights are in hands of service providers who control their usage in their terms of service. But with all the other digital assets, none of the subjects can be sure whether and how the law will apply. The interpretation of the law is thus in the hands of judges potentially deciding over future disputes

Unclear Possibility of Acquiring Ownership

A further potential issue with current traditional property law is that it does not explicitly recognize any method of acquiring ownership. The process of acquiring ownership may also differ based on individual digital assets. For example, the considerations will differ if we analyse the mining process of bitcoins, their purchase through an exchange, or if we evaluate how ownership can be acquired when registering on a social media page. In any case, the law does not have a clear answer to any of these outlined processes.

As discussed in Chapter 4, one possibility of acquiring ownership is through appropriation. In this regard, an alteration to the current civil code is required to make it is clear that a digital nature is not an obstacle when it comes to the acquisition of ownership, especially in relation to the institute of appropriation. This change might make the application of traditional property rights possible, at least to some digital assets such as AI-generated artworks or cryptoassets obtained through mining which usually do not belong to anyone. Furthermore, the explicit possibility of acquiring ownership through the creation of a new thing, which would align the law with legal theory, may open the possibility for more digital assets to become the object of ownership.

---

[467] PERZANOWSKI, Aaron a Jason M SCHULTZ. *The End of Ownership: Personal Property in the Digital Economy*. Cambridge: The MIT Press, 2016. ISBN 0-262-33596-4, p. 20.

The Interplay between Digital Assets and Copyrighted Works

Some digital assets (such as in-game objects or social media accounts) are either wholly or partly protected by intellectual property law. As a result, these digital assets are usually governed by license agreements which do not confer any rights to users.[468] From a legal standpoint, it is currently unclear whether the parallel use of traditional property and intellectual property is possible. As will be discussed below, it appears that under Czech law, the application of property rights to those digital assets that are protected by copyright is not possible. Nevertheless, this does not preclude the possibility that these digital assets may be considered things and that other provisions may be applied.

Two separate issues concern copyrighted works. The first is the question of whether a copyrighted work can be a thing. Second, if it is a thing, to what extent do provisions governing "things" apply to them? Moreover, can we apply all such provisions, or should we exclude property rights?

As Chapter 4 demonstrated, the answer to the first question is in the affirmative. Based on the recent commentaries to the Czech Civil Code, copyrighted works are things.[469] What poses an interpretational problem, however, is the legal consequences of categorizing copyrighted works as things.

The first issue is whether property rights are attached to copyrighted works. In the early 2000s, Fairfield considered whether the law allows for an overlap of both rights for the same object.[470] He argued that the ownership of a physical carrier like a book by itself does not negate intellectual property rights, since the owner cannot infringe these rights by, for example, copying the content. Therefore, the same should apply for intangible things as well.[471] There is certainly merit to this argument, since restrictions on the bundle of rights for physical copies usually only applies to acts that infringe copyright. The issue is that European copyright law treats intangible objects differently to tangible ones, especially in the case of second sales and transfers, as confirmed in the CJEU decisions Tom Kabinet[472] and Used-Soft.[473] Moreover, the limitations put on users through EULAs such as a prohibition on transfers go beyond what is normally required in the case of physical carriers.

Furthermore, it appears that the Czech Civil Code itself excludes the possibility of one object being subject to both traditional property and intellectual property rights. Although it is not explicitly addressed whether some objects may be

---

[468] DIMITA, Gaetano, LEE Yin Harn et al. IP and Metaverse(S) — an Externally Commissioned Research Report. Queen Mary Law Research Paper no. 427/2024. [online] February 2024 [Accessed 2024-05-02] Available at: https://papers.ssrn.com/sol3/papers.cfm?abstract_id=4756583, pp. 26–27; PAŁKA, Przemysław. Virtual Property — Towards a General Theory. 2017, pp. 47–49.

[469] For further analysis, see Chapter 4.1.1.

[470] FAIRFIELD, Joshua. Virtual Property. *Boston University Law Review*. 2005, vol. 85, no. 4, p. 1096 and following.

[471] Ibid.

[472] Judgment of the European Court of Justice from 19 December 2019, C-263/18.

[473] Judgment of the European Court of Justice from 3 July 2012, C-128/11.

protected by both intellectual property laws and as traditional property, the parallel application of both traditional property and intellectual property principles is excluded, since property rights to copyrighted works are governed by the Copyright Act.[474] This approach was only reinforced via the implementation of the Digital Content Directive. As Chapter 3 demonstrated, the notions of digital assets and digital content are essentially interchangeable, as both cover almost the same category of digital objects. Therefore, some of the types of digital assets and digital content are copyrighted works. Legislators thus had to deal with cases when digital content provided to consumers was protected by intellectual property rights. As a result, the use of digital content protected by intellectual property is governed by licenses.[475] Consequently, its use is limited by the given license.

Moreover, what Fairfield did not consider are the multiple paradoxes caused by the parallel use of property rights and intellectual property. Digital assets protected by intellectual property are typically licensed to users with a limited scope of use. No transfer of title occurs — and even if it did, the license scope under the Czech Civil Code is limited to "*uses known at the time of the license*".[476] On top of that, intellectual property law and traditional property law, among others, offer multiple legal protections which the law subjects may use in order to protect their interests. However, this protection works on a mutually exclusive basis. If a user owns their in-game objects, they may use proprietary claims to protect them. This in general excludes the possibility of a service provider to use their IP protection, as this IP protection may limit how the user uses the given in-game object. Therefore, both protections cannot apply at the same time.

Even the parallel application of both traditional property and intellectual property still leads to numerous gaps and inconsistencies. The only way both protections can partially work is if the relationship between a service provider and user is covered under intellectual property, while the user's protection against other third parties applies within a traditional property framework. This form of protection may still be applicable today. Since possession is not a property right, it is possible to conclude that users would have digital assets in their possession and, as a result, could use a claim against a third party, for which the Czech Civil Code allows.[477]

The UK Law Commission presumes that the discussion on whether digital assets that are protected by copyright will also address property rights.[478] Accordingly, legislators should consider whether it would be beneficial to explicitly address the legal

[474] TOMÍŠEK, Jan. Software jako věc v režimu nového občanského zákoníku. *Revue pro právo a technologie.* 2014, vol. 5, no. 9.

[475] Section 2389a, Czech Civil Code.

[476] Section 2372 paragraph 1, Czech Civil Code.

[477] TOMÍŠEK, Jan. Software jako věc v režimu nového občanského zákoníku. *Revue pro právo a technologie*. 2014, vol. 5, no. 9, p. 204; Section 1003, Czech civil code.

[478] UK LAW COMMISSION. Digital Assets Consultation Paper. [online] 28. 7. 2022 [Accessed 2024-05-20]. Available at: https://cloud-platform-e218f50a4812967ba1215eaecede923f.s3.amazonaws.com/uploads/sites/30/2022/07/Digital-Assets-Consultation-Paper-Law-Commission-1.pdf, pp. 136–137.

consequences of categorizing a copyrighted work as a thing under the Civil Code. To give an example, should the fact that an in-game object is protected by copyright mean that the users will always be limited by a license's terms and can never gain full control over the object or use a property protection principle against a third party? Or if traditional property rights do not apply, what other provisions do? And to what extent? It is essential to address these underlying questions in a clear and transparent manner within the law itself.

Traditional Property and Intangible World

Historically, the system of traditional property law was built for tangible objects and the tangible world. As a result, some jurisdictions do not recognize intangible things at all. And although it can be argued that Roman law recognized intangible things, it was emphasized that intangible things under Roman law were rights and not intangible objects.[479] Furthermore, past interpretations also stated that analogies of digital assets with tangible things were not valid, thus necessitating a further examination of the differences and similarities between tangible and intangible things.[480]

Many examples in the Czech Civil Code illustrate that the system of property law was built for the tangible world. For example, the code contains provisions that deal with ownership in the case of alluvium[481], or a detailed description of how one may acquire ownership of securities.[482] Yet the code does not address a single situation when it comes to digital assets. Similarly, even commentators rarely address digital assets. Looking into such commentaries, intangible things, and the rights associated with them, are often described through examples such as claims or trade secrets. Nevertheless, substantial differences exist between a claim and an example of a digital asset. Consequently, the conclusions drawn for these intangible things cannot be analogically used for digital assets.

Furthermore, these examples are just a small demonstration of a far bigger issue — namely that traditional property ownership is about an absolute legal dominion under which one may control tangible things and exclude others.[483] However, an absolute legal dominion over digital assets in the cyberspace is rarely possible. This may be due either to limitations set in the respective terms of service, or in the way that technical infrastructure works, or both. This is something that should be addressed on a conceptual level by legislators. Either the requirement for control and/or legal dominion is such a strong defining feature of things/property/ownership

[479] PAŁKA, Przemysław. *Virtual Property — Towards a General Theory*. 2017, p. 149.

[480] CHAN, Timothy. "The nature of property in cryptoassets." Online. *Legal studies (Society of Legal Scholars)*. 2023, vol. 43, no. 3, p. 482.

[481] Section 1066 and following of the Czech Civil Code.

[482] Section 1103 and 1104 of the Czech Civil Code.

[483] MAYDANYK, Roman, MAYDANYK, Nataliia and Nataliia POPOVA. Reconsidering the Concept of a Thing in Terms of the Digital Environment: Law Towards an Understanding of a Digital Thing. Online. *Open Journal for Legal Studies (Online)*. [online] 2022 [Accessed 2024-04-12]. Available at: https://centerprode.com/ojls/ojls0502/coas.ojls.0502.01031m.pdf, p. 35.

(or whatever any legal system calls it) and therefore, the concept of ownership cannot be applied to digital assets; or, given the nature of digital assets and intangible things in general, the requirement for control may be stretched so as to accommodate the digital world.

5.2 Regulatory Challenges

The discussion surrounding digital assets often merges conceptual and regulatory aspects, which in itself has been subject to criticism.[484] However, with such an uncertain legal framework, it is only natural that the conceptual and regulatory debates overlap. Ultimately, viable application is heavily reliant on its interpretation. And the interpretation will always be affected by the given author's opinion on the merits combined with their values.

The aim of this subchapter is not to draft actual provisions for legislators, but to offer guidance on what conceptual and regulatory questions policymakers should ask and what challenges should be overcome. Three main issues will be addressed. First, whether the law should cover the broad notion of digital assets as one or focus on specific digital assets separately. Second, which legal framework should be applicable to digital assets and should it comprise any of the currently existing ones. Third, whether policymakers should regulate the current practices of service providers. The paradox here is that all three questions are interconnected, and it is not clear which should be answered first and which last.

5.2.1 The Conceptualisation of the Notion of Digital Assets

The most apparent regulatory challenge is how the law should conceptualize digital assets in the first place, especially since understandings of the notion may differ based on the context or based on the particular body or authority using the term. This is well illustrated by the recent UNIDROIT Principles, which appear tailored to cryptoassets more than to a broad category of digital assets. Similarly, although the UK Law Commission examined digital assets as a broad category, the conclusion stemming from their consultation is that only cryptoassets attract property rights.[485]

[484] PAŁKA, Przemysław. *Virtual Property — Towards a General Theory*. 2017, p. 18.

[485] DIMITA, Gaetano, LEE Yin Harn et al. IP and Metaverse(S) — an Externally Commissioned Research Report. *Queen Mary Law Research Paper no. 427/2024.* [online] February 2024 [Accessed 2024-05-02] Available at: https://papers.ssrn.com/sol3/papers.cfm?abstract_id=4756583, p. 27.

In all cases, the definite conclusion is that the legal framework for digital assets is uncertain, and a need exists to clear up which rights apply and to what extent. However, in order to that, it must first be determined which digital assets are covered in the given definition and the respective legal framework. If the assessment is about whether one umbrella term should provide traditional property law protections, the answer might be different than if the starting point is that a completely new legal framework needs to be created. Since this book is about traditional property, the following paragraphs only discuss the situation in relation to traditional property. Here legislators have three options for how to deal with the current state.

First, legislators can make amendments to property law for digital assets as a broad, umbrella category. This means adopting a broad definition on the notion and analysing the legal consequences for dozens of individual digital assets. Such an umbrella term would have to accommodate various different digital assets and be adequately future-proof. And with some digital assets, the application of traditional property simply will not work.

Alternatively, legislators can either narrow down the definition to include only certain digital assets, which would either share some similar features, or for which legislators would envision the application of traditional property. This means identifying which digital assets require changes and which do not. On the one hand this alternative means that the legal framework would not cover all digital assets; on the other, it would be a way to prevent too broad an application. Similarly, it would leave the possibility open to alter certain user rights under a different legal framework (such as consumer protection).

The third option would be to maintain the *status quo* and to let court practice deal with issues that arise via each individual case. However, I personally do not find this solution to be sustainable. The legal uncertainty inherent in the current legal framework, coupled with Schulz's and Perzanowski's argument that the lack of ownership in digital assets may result in a widening of the social gaps between different social groups[486] are strong enough grounds to provide a definitive answer to this decades-long question.

I would argue in favour of the second solution. Digital assets are not a homogeneous group. While "digital assets" may be useful as an umbrella term outside of the law, its broadness makes the application of the law challenging. The difficulty in applying a single legal definition to all digital assets arises from the fact that different digital assets fulfil different legal definitions. This is due to several factors. Firstly, each digital asset operates within a different technical infrastructure. An essential difference exists between how cryptoassets work and are offered (even inside this specific subgroup) and how social media accounts operate. This means that presently a detailed interpretation of the nature of each digital asset is required each time the existing legal framework is applied; and we are still unable to reach

[486] PERZANOWSKI, Aaron a Jason M SCHULTZ. *The End of Ownership: Personal Property in the Digital Economy*. Cambridge: The MIT Press, 2016. ISBN 0-262-33596-4, p. 170.

a definitive conclusion about whether property rights (or any other rights) apply to them as a whole group.

Secondly, each digital asset presents a unique legal challenge due to conflicting legislation. For instance, some digital assets are partially or fully protected by intellectual property laws, while others exist in a legal grey area with no regulation at all. Therefore, it appears impossible to unify all of what is colloquially understood to be digital assets into one category. Moreover, a risk will always exist that with new technologies emerging applicable categories will become obsolete.

Additionally, significant differences are found in how distinct digital assets function. For example, AI-generated works can be used by users for various purposes, while control over social media accounts is limited. Similarly, it is easy to trade cryptoassets, but in virtual worlds and videogames, the transfer of in-game goods is often limited by game developers.

The above leads me to the conclusion that we can never truly incorporate all digital assets into one umbrella term. Furthermore, what is often proposed to be covered through legal protections are those digital assets that allow for investment, and thus the value that is being protected is the money invested. But this means that a significant market segment (like virtual worlds or social media) remains overlooked.[487]

Based on the above considerations, I find it important to regulate digital assets on a case-by-case basis, tailored to the specific needs and characteristics of each asset. Different digital assets may require different regulations based on their unique features and purposes. Some may require investment and/or consumer protections. Others may simply provide users with greater rights to their content. Which may lead to notions concerning digital assets being entirely sidelined. However, since the umbrella term has never really worked for anything more than demonstrating the "bigger picture" of issues relating to rights to online content, this may actually be beneficial.

Furthermore, digital assets should in any case be examined by legislators on a more interdisciplinary basis. While it is important to, for example, examine digital assets from the point-of-view of traditional property laws, the UK Law Commission's Consultation shows us that a one-sided analysis might not fulfil its goals if it omits other legal frameworks. Consequently, applicable laws such as the Data Act, GDPR, MiCA or Copyright Act must also be taken into consideration.

[487] Comp. MACDONALD, Michaela. Digital Assets and Value. Presentation. 5. 3. 2024. QMIPRI Workshop on Digital Assets.

5.2.2 Should Traditional Property Law Governs Digital Assets?

As this work has demonstrated, the applicability of a traditional property framework to digital assets is not just a theoretical question, as recently the courts have actually allowed for such an application. Moreover, the application of traditional property may, in some cases, provide users with needed protections for their digital assets, as we have seen in cases dealing with cryptoassets. To this extent, it is logical to apply the traditional property framework, as it offers users legal instruments that may protect their digital assets.

Similarly, there are merits to the argument that users should have similar rights to both their tangible and intangible things. However, the question we should be asking is whether traditional property principles are *suitable* for the digital world and whether another system could be a better fit. A possible alternative is the quasi-property system suggested by Hummel and Braun, built on the possibility to "*distribute, retract, shield and share*."[488]

On the one hand, property is a category only formalized by law, but which stems from the needs of society and the market in order to allow for the transfer and effective allocation of resources.[489] This is why we can look at property as a "creature of the law" with no naturally inherent property rights.[490] Consequently, what may fall into the category of a thing, be it a tangible or intangible object, remains a legal construct.[491] It is therefore up to legislators to establish digital assets within the category of a thing (or not). This can be achieved either through direct amendments to the law (namely the Civil Code) or by offering an interpretation that would allow for such an application within the limits of current laws. The latter, for example, was the path taken by the UK Law Commission via their Consultation Paper[492] supporting the idea of a so-called "third category of thing". This being said, even though the document provided a possible viable interpretation for the existing framework, the UK Law Commission still argued that some statutory law changes would be necessary in order to ensure legal certainty.[493]

---

488 HUMMEL, Patrik, Matthias BRAUN a Peter DABROCK. Own Data? Ethical Reflections on Data Ownership. *Philosophy & Technology*. 2021, vol. 34, no. 3, p. 554.

489 MACDONALD, Michaela. *The Case for Virtual Property*. Dissertation thesis. Queen Mary University of London, 2016, pp. 181–182.

490 RAHMATIAN, Andreas. Debts, Money, Intellectual Property, Data and the Concept of Dematerialised Property. *Journal of Intellectual Property, Information Technology and Electronic Commerce Law*. 2020, vol. 11, no. 2, p. 188.

491 Ibid.

492 UK LAW COMMISSION. Digital Assets Consultation Paper. [online] 28. 7. 2022 [Accessed 2023-07-20]. Available at: https://cloud-platform-e218f50a4812967ba1215eaecede923f.s3.amazonaws.com/uploads/sites/30/2022/07/Digital-Assets-Consultation-Paper-Law-Commission-1.pdf.

493 UK LAW COMMISSION. Digital Asset: Final Report. [online] 27. 6. 2023 [Accessed 2024-05-20]. Available at: https://cloud-platform-e218f50a4812967ba1215eaecede923f.s3.amazonaws.com/uploads/sites/30/2023/06/Final-digital-assets-report-FOR-WEBSITE-2.pdf, p. 22.

But even if we apply traditional property, the application is merely theoretical and not factual. In reality, users will often not have any control over their digital assets simply because service providers (either by contract or by the design of the respective platform) will not allow for any basic property-based functions to apply. Additionally, in the case of transfers, a requirement for access information will often exist. Which means a kind of paradox — even though it may allow for such an application, in reality it is factually impossible to exercise these rights. This is why any changes to the law that would make such an application clear must also consider the extent to which property rights might interfere with the current practices of service providers, and whether property rights would even apply to those digital assets governed by contracts. This brings us back to the initial question regarding the delineation of digital assets that should be subject to regulation.

Even more conceptual obstacles to the application of property rights can be found. In addition to the difficulty of precisely defining the object of a right due to the complex data structure of digital assets, other issues exist, such as the ambiguous content of the given right or the manner in which it is acquired or transferred.[494] These all must be addressed where digital assets are governed under property law principles. However, given the complexity of issues and the specific nature of digital assets — including the right of access, control, and the transfer of the desired bundle of rights — it would, arguably, make more sense to introduce a new system of *quasi-property* or *sui generis* rights for digital assets. Since it is often just particular rights that are of concern and not the entire ownership *per se*, such a system would be tailored specifically for digital assets and could provide users with an adequate bundle of rights.[495]

Similarly, an incidental categorization of property can be found within the Czech Civil Code. This would not require a new system to be created. In this case, some property rights or proprietary protections would apply to digital assets while other provisions would be explicitly excluded. For example, given the importance of *rei vindicatio* claims, as illustrated by the recent cases discussed in Chapter 4, the code may contain an explicit provision that allows for intangibles to be recovered.

To conclude, a tendency exists to apply a traditional property law framework to at least some digital assets such as cryptoassets. However, based on the high number of authors seeking to determine the exact object of property rights and examine every detail of how digital assets could be controlled, one cannot escape the inevitable conclusion that they are seeking to delay the obvious — namely that traditional property simply does not fit into the virtual world because it was never meant to govern it. And thus, a new, more suitable framework must be created instead. Unlike in the UK, currently no systematic regulatory discussions are taking place about the

494 RAHMATIAN, Andreas. Debts, Money, Intellectual Property, Data and the Concept of Dematerialised Property. *Journal of Intellectual Property, Information Technology and Electronic Commerce Law.* 2020, vol. 11, no. 2, p. 192.

495 HUMMEL, Patrik, Matthias BRAUN a Peter DABROCK. Own Data? Ethical Reflections on Data Ownership. *Philosophy & Technology*. 2021, vol. 34, no. 3, p. 554.

application of property rights to digital assets. An opportunity existed to raise the debate during the implementation of the Digital Content Directive; but even if a debate occurred within the implementing body, it never reached a wider professional audience. As a result, the concept of digital content (and digital services) under Czech law remains difficult to grasp.

Notwithstanding the above, until a clear legal framework is created for digital assets, the protections offered though property law is logical to apply. Because traditional property law is the only applicable framework that presently gives users the desired rights and protections.

5.2.3 To What Extent Should We Regulate Service Providers?

Presently, service providers have sole control over digital assets, and limit their use through their respective terms of service.[496] The final challenge for regulation is whether it should target service providers' practices of limiting users' rights to digital assets and instead allow users to gain more control. This issue does not apply to all digital assets; it only applies to those that are provided as a service, or as part of a service, or are part of larger infrastructure provided to the user, such as social media accounts, in-game objects or e-books. As the analysis of Czech traditional property law demonstrated, classifying these types of digital assets as a thing presents significant interpretational challenges, given that they are typically protected by intellectual property or carry a notable privacy aspect. Consequently, for example, social media accounts are not a thing according to Czech civil law, and thus users do not have any rights to them.

This opens up a question of whether legislators should provide users with a new framework under which service providers would be obliged to provide users with certain rights. These do not necessarily have to be property rights. In the end, the framework might be something similar to the Data Act's duty to allow for interoperability. Here, legislators did not establish any new proprietary rights for users (or "customers", as per the Data Act's terminology), but only created a duty to transfer digital elements to another provider. Therefore, it is not unthinkable that regulators may introduce something similar to tackle common issues faced by users, such as the lack of opportunity to transfer the rights to an account or the possibility to inherit it. This solution may be in line with the quasi-property approach referenced in the previous subchapter.

In the end, the core question is who should have the final authority to determine the rights and limitations of users — the law or the terms of service? I believe this is the final challenge that remains to be solved by policy makers.

---

[496] MICHELS, Johan David a MILLARD, Christopher. The New Things: Property Rights in Digital Files?. *Cambridge Law Journal*. 2022, vol. 81, no. 2, p. 287.

5.3 Final Remarks

The second part of this chapter began with three interconnected issues. First, whether digital assets should be regulated as one homogenous category under the law. Second, whether the traditional property law is the optimal legal framework. And third, whether regulations should override current service provider practices.

The category of intangible things is rarely analysed in connection to digital assets, even though it is an ideal category to provide property rights to users in possession of digital assets.

I find the logical solution here is not to push for a definitive interpretation, but to accommodate the law to fit the virtual world. This can be achieved even with small changes to the existing legal framework. For example, if the property law framework is desirable, we can simply adapt it so that it introduces a pledge register for intangible things or creates a system in which one can inherit intangibles.

A need exists to establish a legal framework for digital assets. However, the exact scope of the framework (i.e. which digital assets it should cover), or what kind of rights and obligations it would address, is up to policymakers. Lawmakers have numerous potential solutions which they could propose in this respect.

The first possibility is to protect digital assets as traditional property. For example, if lawmakers deem traditional property protections adequate, a slight change to existing provisions must be made. Here, I would suggest that the understanding of control within ownership should be broadened so as to acknowledge the nature of digital assets which cannot be controlled in the same manner as tangible things.

Similarly, although it may not be clear how, for example, a digital asset would be reivindicated, or how it should be described as a clear object, the law should embrace this technical complexity and at least allow for the application of these institutes. The rest can be dealt with pragmatically on a case-by-case basis.

Policymakers may, of course, decide to go in another direction and create a quasi-property framework for digital assets. In the end, creating a new *sui generis* framework or allowing digital assets to function within the existing system is just a one part of the solution. This is because it would only address only those digital assets whose use is not restricted by terms of service.

To conclude, the application of current traditional property law is like flipping a coin. Although legislators clearly had well-meaning intentions to introduce a broad category of a thing, the wording of the current provisions leads to multiple interpretational possibilities. Consequently, the intention of lawmakers can be overturned by a court deciding in favour of either interpretation. Therefore, a need still exists to clarify the legal framework, which remains a task for Czech lawmakers.

CONCLUSION

The topic of digital assets and property law often stirs controversy. For some, the idea of ownership of anything digital is simply out of question and no arguments presented will change their mind as it is determined by the current property discourse that data cannot be owned. For others, ownership is seen as empowerment and a way how to give consumers power over what should belong to them. And then one can encounter those who argue for a new legal framework, similar to ownership, which could solve the issue once and for all. But for the cost of creating a completely new institute.

There is a paradox that on one hand, the digital economy led to creation of very valuable economy. And on the other hand, lawyers struggle to determine who actually owns the primary object of this economy. Presently, we can observe a number of new regulations that have come into force, such the Data Act, MiCA or the Digital Content Directive — all adopted with a view to facilitating digital intangibles. At the same time, Digital Services Act introduced a new regulatory framework for platforms which are often used to store the digital assets. However, none of these specifically addresses the issue of the property rights to digital assets, nor does it provide a complex legal framework to govern the rights to digital assets while providing legal protections for users. This can be seen as a definite answer that no digital intangibles ownership is coming, unless the intangibles act more like traditional property objects and can be factually controlled. Yet, we can see impulses from different parts of the world that the debate is not over yet as evident with the recent publication of the UK Law Commission's Consultation and the UNIDROIT Principles. Furthermore, the possibility of using proprietary protections to recover cryptoassets was recently granted in the UK, Singapore and the Czech Republic. This can be seen as a first signals that the protection of digital assets through property law is not a far-fetched concept at all.

This monograph focused on the current relativisation of property concepts and examined whether a legal system that recognises intangible things could allow for the application of property rights to digital assets, or whether boundaries still apply that prevent application. The aim of the monograph was to examine the bigger picture and address the differences between individual digital assets in relation to property rights.

Digital assets constitute a broad heterogeneous group. Therefore, it was necessary to first examine the notion itself and to put it into perspective with other similar notions such as virtual property, cryptoassets, digital content and data that is also subject to regulatory discussion. The analysis in Chapter 3 demonstrated that we can come across a variety of notions in this respect — albeit largely meaning the same. The only difference is the context in which the given notion is used. While the concept of virtual property is often connected to virtual worlds and user rights to their in-game objects, the notion of digital assets often appears in relation to property rights and the inheritance of either cryptoassets or social media accounts. Similarly, in the context of consumer protection, the term "digital content" is used. Ultimately, digital assets can be characterized as a digital intangible in a specific form which poses a value to the user. Moreover, their specific form is what distinguishes them from raw data. However, this conclusion is only derived from legal literature and soft-law instruments. This is why it would be beneficial to harmonise the terminology used in the law, which would in turn help to create a clear, unified legal framework as opposed to the current fragmented one.

This work also explored the limitations of Czech property laws and the ways in which these gaps could be overcome through legislative change. The general findings are that even though the body of Czech property law recognizes intangible things, the application to digital assets faces multiple limitations stemming from the law itself, such as the limited possibility to apply property rights to digital assets under Section 979 of the Czech Civil Code. It is also unclear how ownership of digital assets is acquired. Finally, the degree of benefit of recognising certain digital assets as things (where we cannot ultimately apply property law) should be made clear.

Furthermore, research has shown that we cannot conclude that every digital asset will have the same legal nature. The analysis demonstrated that while cryptoassets will meet the requirements to be recognised as a thing, social media accounts do not fall into the category of a thing due to their complex technological infrastructure, personal nature and applicable contractual protections.

As discussed in Chapter 5, property rights are a legal construct entirely in the hands of legislators, who have the discretion to decide what exactly will benefit from property protections. Consequently, gaps in the legal system should be addressed by policy makers. If the intention is to include intangible things in the property system, the civil Code should reflect this in more detail. This would remove the current legal uncertainty for both users and service providers. In addition, legislators should consider whether rights to digital assets should be regulated under a separate legal framework. It is clear that property law cannot currently be applied to digital assets without careful interpretation. Moreover, given the complex nature of digital assets, it is often unclear what exactly should be covered by property rights. Therefore, the creation of a new functional framework similar to property rights would be an appropriate solution and could overcome the difficulty currently faced when determining the object of protection.

Although this book has drawn a number of conclusions, its scope is limited to property rights. Accordingly, numerous issues in this field remain to be discussed and explored. Digital assets (or however they are termed) are subject to many regulations. Resolving the issue of the respective protections from a property law perspective will also require compliance with other laws. Similarly, given the differences that exist between the wide variety of digital assets, a need exists to decide for which assets protections are beneficial and for which they are not. This is something that future research could address. Arguably, the creation of a new legal framework that would adapt to digital assets would be a major step in the right direction and represent a significant change to current laws. However, as users have not only a sentimental but also monetary value in their digital assets, it may be necessary to properly protect them — as considerable uncertainty presently exists about whether proprietary protections apply. Indeed, until the existing legal framework is clarified, the interpretation of the body of property law in favour of its application to digital assets remains a viable and indeed necessary possibility.

BIBLIOGRAPHY

ALI-ELI. Principles for a Data Economy. [online] 2021 [Accessed 2023-05-22]. Available at: https://www.europeanlawinstitute.eu/fileadmin/user_upload/p_eli/Publications/ALI-ELI_Principles_for_a_Data_Economy_Final_Council_Draft.pdf.

ALLEN, Jason G.; Rauchs, Michel; BLANDIN, Apolline; BEAR, Keith. Legal and Regulatory Considerations for Digital Assets. [online] [Accessed 2023-05-23]. Available at: https://www.jbs.cam.ac.uk/wp-content/uploads/2020/10/2020-ccaf-legal-regulatory-considerations-report.pdf.

ALLEN, Jason. Property in Digital Coins. *European Property Law Journal*. 2019, vol. 8, no. 1.

ASHFORD, Kate and ADAMS, Michael. What Is Bitcoin And How Does It Work? *Forbes*. [online] 8 June 2022 [Accessed 2024-02-16] Available at: https://www.forbes.com/advisor/investing/cryptocurrency/what-is-bitcoin/.

BANTA, Natalie. Inherit the Cloud: The Role of Private Contracts in Distributing or Deleting Digital Assets at Death. *Fordham Law Review*, vol. 83, no. 2.

BANTA, Natalie. Property interests in digital assets: The rise of digital feudalism. *Cardozo Law Review*. 2016, vol. 38, no. 3.

BARONE, Adam. What Is an Asset? Definition, Types, and Examples. *Investopedia*. [online] 29. 3. 2023 [Accessed 2023-05-17] Available at: https://www.investopedia.com/terms/a/asset.asp.

BIRNHACK, Michael a MORSE, Tal. Digital remains: property or privacy? Online. *International journal of law and information technology*. 2022, vol. 30, no. 3.

BLAZER, Charles. Blockchains and Digital Assets. *Pierce Law Review*. 2006, vol. 5, no. 1.

BUŘÍNSKÁ. Barbora. Digitální dědictví řeší málokdo, přitom může ukrývat miliony. *Novinky.cz*. [online] 1. 11. 2022 [Accessed 2023-10-26]. Available at: https://www.novinky.cz/clanek/finance-digitalni-dedictvi-resi-malokdo-pritom-muze-ukryvat-miliony-40412525.

BYGRAVE, Lee. Information Concepts in Law: Generic Dreams and Definitional Daylight. *Oxford Journal of Legal Studies*. 2015, vol. 35, no. 1.

CASTRONOVA, Edward. Virtual Worlds: A First-Hand Account of Market and Society on the Cyberian Frontier. CESifo Working Paper. 2001, (618).

CIFRINO, Christopher J. Virtual Property, Virtual Rights: Why Contract Law, Not Property Law, Must Be the Governing Paradigm in the Law of Virtual Worlds. *B.C. L. REV*. 2014, vol. 55, no. 1.

COMPUTER SECURITY RESOURCE CENTRE. Digital Asset. [online] [Accessed 2023-05-17]. Available at: https://csrc.nist.gov/glossary/term/digital_asset.

CONNOR, John. Digital Life after Death: The Issue of Planning for a Person's Digital Assets after Death. *Estate Planning & Community Property Law Journal*. 2011, no. 2.

Digital Assets. *Gartner Glossary*. [online] [Accessed 2023-05-17]. Available at: https://www.gartner.com/en/finance/glossary/digital-assets.

DIMITA, Gaetano, LEE Yin Harn et al. IP and Metaverse(S) - an Externally Commissioned Research Report. Queen Mary Law Research Paper no. 427/2024. [online] February 2024 [Accessed 2024-05-02] Available at: https://papers.ssrn.com/sol3/papers.cfm?abstract_id=4756583.

DVOŘÁK, Jan, Jiří ŠVESTKA et al. *Občanské právo hmotné 3*. Praha: Wolters Kluwer, 2015. ISBN 978-80-7478-935-9.

ENG, Kenneth W. Content Creators, Virtual Goods: Who Owns Virtual Property. *Cardozo Arts & Entertainment Law Journal*. 2016, vol. 34, no. 1.

ERLANK, Wian. Don't Touch My Virtual Property: Justifications for the Recognition of Virtual Property, *S. AFRICAN L.J.* 2016, vol. 133, no. 3.

ERLANK, Wian. Lecture: Introduction to Virtual Property. [online] 2009 [Accessed 2023-05-24]. Available at: https://papers.ssrn.com/sol3/papers.cfm?abstract_id=1491118.

ERP, Sjef van and SWINNEN, Koen, 2022, The legal status of co-generated data. *Technology and Regulation*. 13 June 2022. Vol. 2022.

ERP, Sjef van. Ownership of Data: The Numerus Clausus of Legal Objects. *Brigham-Kanner Property Rights Conference Journal*. 2017, volume 6. Revised and expanded version.

EUROPEAN COMMISSION. An EU initiative on Web 4.0 and virtual worlds: a head start in the next technological transition. {COM(2023) 442 final}. 2023.

EUROPEAN LAW INSTITUTE. ELI Principles on the Use of Digital Assets as Security. [online] 28. 7. 2022 [Accessed 2023-07-20]. Available at: https://www.europeanlawinstitute.eu/fileadmin/user_upload/p_eli/Publications/ELI_Principles_on_the_Use_of_Digital_Assets_as_Security.pdf.

Explanatory Memorandum to the Amendment of the Czech Civil Code. Sněmovní tisk č. 994, p. 84. [online] [Accessed 2023-11-29]. Available at: https://www.psp.cz/sqw/text/orig2.sqw?idd=181044.

Explanatory Memorandum of Czech Civil Code. [online] [Accessed 2023-09-15]. Available at: http://obcanskyzakonik.justice.cz/images/pdf/Duvodova-zprava-NOZ-konsolidovana-verze.pdf.

FAIRFIELD, Joshua. Bitproperty. *Southern California Law Review*. 2014, vol. 88, no. 4.

FAIRFIELD, Joshua. *Owned: Property, Privacy, and the New Digital Serfdom*. Cambridge: Cambridge University Press, 2017.

FAIRFIELD, Joshua. Tokenized: The Law of Non-Fungible Tokens and Unique Digital Property. *Indiana Law Journal*. 2022, vol. 91, no. 4.

FAIRFIELD, Joshua. Virtual Property. *Boston University Law Review*. 2005, vol. 85, no. 4.

FEDERAL DEPARTMENT OF FINANCE. Factsheet on Blockchain and cryptoassets in the financial sector: Switzerland's pioneering role on the international stage. [online] 24. 1. 2022 [Accessed 2023-11-29]. Available at: https://www.sif.admin.ch/sif/en/home/finanzmarktpolitik/digitalisation-financial-sector/blockchain.html.

FIALA, Roman, DRÁPAL, Ljubomír et al. *Občanský zákoník IV. Dědické právo (§ 1475–1720)*. 2nd edition. Prague: C. H. Beck, 2022, p. 4, marg. no. 13.

FRANKENFIELD, Jake. What is a Digital Assets?. *Investopedia*. [online] 30. 6. 2022 [Accessed 2023-05-17]. Available at: https://www.investopedia.com/terms/d/digital-asset-framework.asp.

GOLDBERG, Adam et al. How Are Digital Assets Regulated in the United States and Elsewhere?. *Pillsbury*. [online] 17. 1. 2023 [Accessed 2023-11-29]. Available at: https://www.pillsburylaw.com/en/news-and-insights/digital-assets-regulated-us-elsewhere.html.

GRAZIADEI, Michele and SMITH, Lionel (eds.) *Comparative Property Law*. United Kingdom: Edward Elgar Publishing, 2017. ISBN 9781848447578.

GULLIFER, Louise. English translation of the Mt Gox judgment on the legal status of bitcoin prepared by the Digital Assets Project. [online]. 11. 2. 2019 [Accessed 2023-07-20]. Available at: https://www.law.ox.ac.uk/business-law-blog/blog/2019/02/english-translation-mt-gox-judgment-legal-status-bitcoin-prepared.

HOPKINS, Jamie. Afterlife in the Cloud: Managing a Digital Estate. *Hastings Science and Technology Law Journal*. 2013, vol. 5, no. 2.

HUMMEL, Patrik, Matthias BRAUN a Peter DABROCK. Own Data? Ethical Reflections on Data Ownership. *Philosophy & Technology*. 2021, vol. 34, no. 3.

CHAN, Timothy. The nature of property in cryptoassets. Online. Legal studies (Society of Legal Scholars). 2023, vol. 43, no. 3.

IBÁÑEZ, Luis-Daniel. Blockchains and Digital Assets. EU Blockchain Forum. [online] 2018 [Accessed 2023-05-24]. Available at: https://www.eublockchainforum.eu/sites/default/files/research-paper/blockchains_and_digital_assets_june_version.pdf.

JANOUŠ, Vilém. Digitální dědictví: Uspořádejte svůj odkaz, ať nadobro nezmizí, radí odborníci. *Denik.cz. [*online] 19. 8. 2022 [Accessed 2023-10-26]. Available at: https://www.denik.cz/z_domova/digitalni-dedictvi-20220817.html.

KASTRENAKES, Jacob. Beeple sold an NFT for $69 million. *The Verge*. [online] 24. 6. 2021 [Accessed 2023-03-03]. Available at: https://www.theverge.com/2021/3/11/22325054/beeple-christies-nft-sale-cost-everydays-69-million.

Kazakhstan: New Law Establishes Legal Framework for Digital Assets and Cryptomining. Library of Congress. [online] [Accessed 2023-07-23]. Available at: https://www.loc.gov/item/global-legal-monitor/2023-04-30/kazakhstan-new-law-establishes-legal-framework-for-digital-assets-and-cryptomining/.

KITTEL, David. Dědění Bitcoinu. *Ad Notam*. 2021, no. 2.

KOLÁŘOVÁ, Kateřina. Digitální dědictví zatím neřešíme. *Lidovky.cz*. [online] 28. 11. 2018 [Accessed 2023-10-26]. Available at: https://www.lidovky.cz/byznys/digitalni-dedictvi-zatim-neresime-rika-sef-notarske-komory-neubauer.A181123_142435_ln_byznys_pravo_ssu.

KONEČNÝ, Jaroslav. Non-Fungible Tokens a ochrana spotřebitele. *Revue pro právo a technologie*, 2023, vol. 14, no. 28.

KUNDRÁTOVÁ, Petra and EISENREICH, Jan. Právní aspekty kryptoměn. *AUC Iuridica*. 2018. vol. LXIV, no. 1.

LASTOWKA, Greg — HUNTER, Dan. The Laws of the Virtual Worlds. *California Law Review*. 2004, vol. 92, no. 1.

LAVICKÝ, Petr et al. *Občanský zákoník I. Obecná část* (§ 1–654). 2nd edition. Prague: C. H. Beck, 2022.

LAWRENCE, Dan E. It Really Is Just a Game: The Impracticability of Common Law Property Rights in Virtual Property. *Washburn Law Journal*. 2008, vol. 47, no. 2.

LEHAVI, Amnon. *Property Law in a Globalizing World*. Cambridge University Press, 2019. ISBN 9781108595391.

LEIVA, Daniel. Law of issuance of digital assets in El Salvador. Consortium Legal. [online] [Accessed 2023-07-23]. Available at: https://consortiumlegal.com/en/2023/01/12/law-of-issuance-of-digital-assets-in-el-salvador/.

LEMLEY, Mark A. How Generative AI Turns Copyright Upside Down. [online] June 2023. [Accessed 2024-28-02]. Available at: https://papers.ssrn.com/sol3/papers.cfm?abstract_id=4517702.

LIMBERGOVÁ, Zuzana. Směrnice o digitálním obsahu a jejich implementace v právním řádu ČR. *Revue pro právo a technologie*. 2022, vol. 13, no. 25.

MACDONALD, Michaela. *The Case for Virtual Property*. Dissertation thesis. Queen Mary University of London, 2016.

MACQUEEN, Hector, Charlotte WAELDE, Graeme LAURIE a Abbe BROWN. *Contemporary Intellectual Property.* 2nd. Oxford University Press, 2011. ISBN 978-0-19-957532-9.

MAYDANYK, Roman, MAYDANYK, Nataliia and Nataliia POPOVA. Reconsidering the Concept of a Thing in Terms of the Digital Environment: Law Towards an Understanding of a Digital Thing. *Open Journal for Legal Studies (Online).* [online] 2022 [Accessed 2024-04-12]. Available at: https://centerprode.com/ojls/ojls0502/coas.ojls.0502.01031m.pdf.

MCCARTHY, Laura. Digital Assets and Intestacy. *Boston University Journal of Science and Technology Law*. 2015, vol. 21, no. 2.

MELZER, Filip, TÉGL, Petr et al. *Občanský zákoník: velký komentář.* Svazek III, § 419–653. 2014, p. 243.

MICHELS, Johan David a MILLARD, Christopher. The New Things: Property Rights in Digital Files?. *Cambridge Law Journal*. 2022, vol. 81, no. 2.

MIKK, Tiina, SEIN, Karin. Digital Inheritance: Heirs's Rights to Claim Access to Online Accounts under Estonian Law. *Juridica International*. 2018, vol. 27.

MÍŠEK, Jakub. *Moderní regulatorní metody ochrany osobních údajů*. Brno: MUNI PRESS, 2020. ISBN 978-80-210-9737-7, p. 37–39.

MLADÁ, Klára. (Ne)díla umělé inteligence a počiny dalších (ne)autorů. *Obchodněprávní revue*, 2023, no. 2.

MU, Xiaochen. The challenge of the emergence of virtual property to the traditional legal theory and the corresponding solutions. *European Journal of Law and Technology*. 2023, vol. 14, no. 1.

NEKIT, Kateryna. Social Media Account as an Object of Virtual Property. *Masaryk University Journal of Law and Technology.* 2020, vol. 4, no. 2.

NGAK, Chenda. Couple wins right to view dead child's Facebook account. CBS news. [online] 20 February 2013 [Accessed 2024-02-22]. Available at: https://www.cbsnews.com/news/couple-wins-right-to-view-dead-childs-facebook-account/.

Opinion of the Czech National Bank. K možnosti investičních fondů investovat do kryptoaktiv. [online] 19. 5. 2023 [Accessed 2023-11-29]. Available at: https://www.cnb.cz/cs/dohled-financni-trh/legislativni-zakladna/stanoviska-k-regulaci-financniho-trhu/RS2023-05/.

PAŁKA, Przemysław. *Virtual Property — Towards a General Theory*. 2017.

PATTI, Francesco Paolo, BARTOLINI, Francesca. Digital inheritance and post mortem data protection: The Italian reform. Bocconi Legal Studies Research Paper Series. June 2019, no. 339974.

PERZANOWSKI, Aaron a Jason M SCHULTZ. *The End of Ownership: Personal Property in the Digital Eaconomy.* Cambridge: The MIT Press, 2016. ISBN 0-262-33596-4.

PETROV, Jan, VÝTISK, Michal, BERAN, Vladimír et al. *Občanský zákoník.* 2nd edition. Prague: C. H. Beck, 2023.

POLČÁK, Radim. Informace a data v právu. *Revue pro právo a technologie.* 2016, vol. 7, no. 13.

POLČÁK, Radim. Protiprávní jednání a škoda online. *Bulletin advokacie.* 2021, no. 6.

PURTOVA, Nadezhda. *Property Rights in Personal Data: A European Perspective.* Kluwer Law International, 2012. ISBN 978-90-411-3802-6.

RAHMATIAN, Andreas. Debts, Money, Intellectual Property, Data and the Concept of Dematerialised Property. *Journal of Intellectual Property, Information Technology and Electronic Commerce Law.* 2020, vol. 11, no. 2.

RAMOS, Andy. The metaverse, NFTs and IP rights: to regulate or not to regulate?. [online] June 2022 [Accessed 2023-03-10]. Available at: https://www.wipo.int/wipo_magazine/en/2022/02/article_0002.html.

RAVENSCRAFT, Eric. What Is the Metaverse, Exactly?. *Wired.* [online] 25. 4. 2022 [Accessed 2023-03-03]. Available at: https://www.wired.com/story/what-is-the-metaverse/.

RITTER, Jeffrey a Anna MAYER. Regulating Data as Property: A New Construct for Moving Forward. *Duke Law & Technology Review.* 2018, vol. 16, no. 1.

SOUKUPOVÁ, Jana. Virtuální vlastnictví: problémy spojené s přechodem do virtuálního prostředí z pohledu práva a kritika dosavadního přístupu. *Právník*, vol. 162, no. 2.

SOUKUPOVÁ, Jana. Analysis of the Notion of Digital Assets in the Context of Fragmented Terminology. *The Lawyer Quarterly.* 2024, vol. 14, no. 3.

SPÁČIL, Jiří, KRÁLÍK, Michal et al. *Občanský zákoník III. Věcná práva (§ 976–1474).* 2nd edition. Prague: C. H. Beck, 2021.

STEPHENS, Molly. Sales of In-Game Assets: An Illustration of the Continuing Failure of Intellectual Property Law to Protect Digital-Content Creators. *Texas Law Review.* 2002, vol. 80, no. 6.

SZWAJDLER, Paweł. Digital assets and inheritance law: How to create fundamental principles of digital succession system? *International journal of law and information technology.* 2023, vol. 31, no. 2.

SWINNEN, Koen. Ownership of data: Four recommendations for future research. *Journal of Law, Property, and Society*, vol. 5, no. 3.

ŠVESTKA, Jiří et al. *Občanský zákoník: Komentář, Svazek I, (§ 1–654).* [Systém ASPI]. Wolters Kluwer [Accessed 2023-04-25]. ASPI_ID KO89_a2012CZ. Available at: www.aspi.cz.

ŠVESTKA, Jiří, DVOŘÁK, Jan et al. *Občanský zákoník: Komentář, Svazek III, (§ 976-1474).* [Systém ASPI]. Wolters Kluwer.

Teen steals virtual items, gets real punishment. *CBS.* [online] 31. 1. 2012 [Accessed 2023-07-20]. Available at: https://www.cbsnews.com/news/teen-steals-virtual-items-gets-real-punishment/.

TELEC, Ivo. Držba informací. *Právní rozhledy*, 2014, vol. 4.

TELEC, Ivo. Nový občanský zákoník ve společnosti sítí. *Bulletin advokacie.* [online] 17. 6. 2015. [Accessed 2023-10-31]. Available at: http://www.bulletin-advokacie.cz/novy-obcansky-zakonik-ve-spolecnosti-siti.

TOMÍŠEK, Jan. Software jako věc v režimu nového občanského zákoníku. *Revue pro právo a technologie*. 2014, vol. 5, no. 9.

UK Government. Factsheet: cryptoassets – key terms and definitions. [online] 11. 4. 2023 [Accessed 2023-05-31]. Available at: https://www.gov.uk/government/publications/economic-crime-and-corporate-transparency-bill-2022-factsheets/factsheet-cryptoassets-key-terms-and-definitions.

UK JURISDICTION TASKFORCE. Legal statement on the cryptoasstes and smart contracts. [online] November 2019 [Accessed 2024-02-01] Available at: https://www.blockchain4europe.eu/wp-content/uploads/2021/05/6.6056_JO_Cryptocurrencies_Statement_FINAL_WEB_111119-1.pdf.

UK LAW COMMISSION. Digital Assets Consultation Paper. [online] 28. 7. 2022 [Accessed 2023-07-20]. Available at: https://cloud-platform-e218f50a4812967ba1215eaecede923f.s3.amazonaws.com/uploads/sites/30/2022/07/Digital-Assets-Consultation-Paper-Law-Commission-1.pdf.

UK LAW COMMISSION. Digital Assets: Final Report. [online] 27. 6. 2023 [Accessed 2023-08-31]. Available at: https://cloud-platform-e218f50a4812967ba1215eaecede923f.s3.amazonaws.com/uploads/sites/30/2023/06/Final-digital-assets-report-FOR-WEBSITE-2.pdf.

UNCITRAL. Exploratory work on legal issues related to the digital economy — reports of events. [online] 15. 5. 2020 [Accessed 2023-05-26]. Available at: https://uncitral.un.org/sites/uncitral.un.org/files/media-documents/uncitral/en/v2002569_1.pdf.

UNIDROIT. Principles on Digital Assets and Private Law. [online] September 2023. [Accessed 2023-10-23]. Available at: https://www.unidroit.org/wp-content/uploads/2023/09/Principles-on-Digital-Assets-and-Private-Law.pdf.

VANKÁTOVÁ, Iveta. Digitální dědictví – aneb jak se dědí bitcoin. *Ad Notam*, 2023, vol. 4.

What is an Asset?. *MasterClass*. [online] 7. 6. 2021 [Accessed 2023-05-17]. Available at: https://www.masterclass.com/articles/what-is-an-asset.

What is token? [online] [Accessed 2024-02-16] Available at: https://www.coinbase.com/learn/crypto-basics/what-is-a-token.

WYCZIK, Jakub. The Property Law of Crypto Tokens [online] November 2023 [Accessed 2024-02-01] Available at: SSRN: https://ssrn.com/abstract=4620033 or http://dx.doi.org/10.2139/ssrn.4620033.

ZORICH, Diane. *Introduction to Managing Digital Assets: Options for Cultural and Educational Organizations*. Oxford: Oxford University Press, 1999. ISBN 978-0892365463.

Case Law

Judgement of Supreme Court of New Zealand Jonathan Dixon vs. The Queen SC 82/2014; [2015] NZSC 147 from 25 October 2015.

Judgement of High Court of England from 2019, AA v Persons Unknown, EWHC 3556 English High Court.

Judgement of German Federal Court of Justice from 12 July 2018, AZ III ZR 183/17.

Judgement of High Court of England from 2023 Lavinia Deborah Osbourne v Persons Unknown Category A & Ors [2023] EWHC 39.

Judgement of the Czech Supreme Court 23 Cdo 3320/2020 from 30 August 2021.

Judgement of the Czech Supreme Court 33 Cdo 3720/2020 from 25 November 2021.

Judgement of the Czech Supreme Court 5 Tdo 1085/2017 from 13 December 2017.
Judgement of the Czech Supreme Court NS 22 Cdo 728/2000 from 17 January 2002.
Judgement of the Czech Supreme Court NS 31 Cdo 3375/2015 from 8 March 2017.
Judgement of the European Court of Justice from 19 December 2019, C-263/18.
Judgement of the European Court of Justice from 3 July 2012, C-128/11.
Judgement of the Municipal Court in Prague from 11 October 2023, 10 C 13/2023-16.
Judgement of the Netherlands Commercial Court from 21 April 2023 NCC 22/018.
Judgement of the United States District Court for the District of Columbia from 18 August 2023, Stephen Thaler v. Shira Perlmutter, Civil Action no. 22-1564 (BAH).
Judgement of Tokyo District Court from 2015 Z1 v Mt. Gox, reference number 25541521.
Judgement Your Response v. Datateam Business Media, EWCA Civ 281 from 14 March 2014.

Legislation

Act no. 121/2000 on Copyright and Rights Related to Copyright and on Amendment to Certain Acts (the Copyright Act), as amended.
Act no. 89/2012 the Civil Code, as amended.
Act 90/2012 on Commercial Companies and Cooperatives.
AS 2021 33 Bundesgesetz zur Anpassung des Bundesrechts an Entwicklungen der Technik verteilter elektronischer Register.
Directive (EU) 2019/770 of the European Parliament and of the Council of 20 May 2019 on certain aspects concerning contracts for the supply of digital content and digital services.
Directive (EU) 2019/771 of the European Parliament and of the Council of 20 May 2019 on certain aspects concerning contracts for the sale of goods, amending Regulation (EU) 2017/2394 and Directive 2009/22/EC, and repealing Directive 1999/44/EC.
Directive 2011/83/EU of the European Parliament and of the Council of 25 October 2011 on consumer rights, amending Council Directive 93/13/EEC and Directive 1999/44/EC of the European Parliament and of the Council and repealing Council Directive 85/577/EEC and Directive 97/7/EC of the European Parliament and of the Council Text with EEA relevance.
Proposal for a Regulation of the European Parliament and of the Council on Markets in Crypto-assets, and amending Directive (EU) 2019/1937, COM/2020/593 final.
Regulation of the European Parliament and the Council on harmonised rules on fair access to and use of data (Data Act), COM/2022/68 final.

www.ingramcontent.com/pod-product-compliance
Ingram Content Group UK Ltd.
Pitfield, Milton Keynes, MK11 3LW, UK
UKHW020147290926
15471UKWH00004B/737

9 789403 541099